"Christine Chakoian has been thinking carefully about Christian faith, the church, and it's interface with culture all her life. In this highly readable book full of historical resources, contemporary anecdotes, and compelling personal experience, she reminds us that from the beginning Christians (or 'people of faith') have had to respond to cultural change and that recovering our institutional memories (or 'memory') is one of the keys to a viable future. I'm grateful for this book. It belongs on the shelves of anyone who cares about the future of Christian faith."

—John Buchanan, editor/publisher, *The Christian Century*

"Christine Chakoian provides the church a way forward grounded in lessons learned from the church's struggle from its earliest days to serve faithfully amidst cultural change. This is an important book for a church standing between a past gone and a future not yet revealed."

—Lovett H. Weems Jr., Distinguished Professor of Church Leadership, Wesley Theological Seminary

"In her new book, *Cryptomnesia*, Christine Chakoian has done the church and its sometimes bewildered leaders an immense service. In an era of exponential change and huge challenges, she has invited us out of our nervous panic by reminding us of the gift of our 2,000-year history, a treasury rich in the wisdom of creatively and courageously navigating troubled waters. Chakoian teaches us how to negotiate the non-essentials of our traditions while reaffirming the essentials of our faith as the body and mission of Christ."

—Phil Needham, lecturer, author of *When God Becomes Small*, and retired officer from The Salvation Army

"History does indeed repeat itself, and here Christine Chakoian tells us, pastorally but forcefully, why understanding and employing that fact matters so much right now in our lives as Christians and as church. This is a substantial book, as meaty and useful as it is an instructive pleasure to read."

—Phyllis Tickle, author and lecturer

"*Cryptomnesia* charts a path forward to help the church navigate the disorientation of our times. Rather than clinging simplistically to the conclusions of our past, this book mines our past for the early church's pattern of seeking unity in the midst of turbulence. For those with open ears, this book contains hope for the church."
—Dan Entwistle, Managing Executive Director, United Methodist Church of the Resurrection

"Chakoian patiently and persuasively encourages us to revisit the easy assumption that the church's faith is obsolete. She directs us toward the memory of who and whose we are—a memory we may have forgotten in our information-saturated culture—with the promise that the church was born into circumstances amazingly similar to those we face today. *Cryptomnesia* is a must-read for book groups, seekers, pastors, and all others who yearn to see ourselves and our world in the way that God does."
—Theodore J. Wardlaw, President and Professor of Homiletics, Austin Presbyterian Theological Seminary

"*Cryptomnesia* offers a hopeful reminder that the 'post-Christendom' challenges currently facing the church are not new but are reminiscent of the 'pre-Christendom' challenges experienced and overcome by the early church. Christine Chakoian offers practical encouragement for us to reclaim healthy practices of Christian community, engagement with our culture, and biblical conflict resolution, modeling Christian love for people in the church and the world who are watching us closely."
—Tim Catlett, pastor, Apex UMC Family of Faith Communities

"Christine Chakoian has written a shrewd and suggestive book filled with fresh insight and teeming with rich probes of new possibility for the church. She argues by way of analogy from the early church to the contemporary church, both of which have been called to face immense circumstances of challenge. She articulates parallels between then and now, through which we can draw *comfort* that we have been here before, *wisdom* on how to engage faithfully, and *assurance* that we can cope effectively. Her exposition greatly illuminates our current situation in the church and points the way ahead with the deep challenges of pluralism and decentering."
—Walter Brueggemann, theologian, Old Testament scholar, Columbia Theological Seminary

CRYPTOMNESIA

How a
Forgotten Memory
Could Save the Church

Christine A. Chakoian

✝) Abingdon Press

Nashville

CRYPTOMNESIA:
HOW A FORGOTTEN MEMORY COULD SAVE THE CHURCH

Copyright © 2014 by Abingdon Press

All rights reserved.
No part of this work may be reproduced or transmitted in any form or by any means, electronic or me-
chanical, including photocopying and recording, or by any information storage or retrieval system, except
as may be expressly permitted by the 1976 Copyright Act or in writing from the publisher. Requests for
permission should be addressed to Permissions, Abingdon Press, P.O. Box 801, 201 Eighth Avenue South,
Nashville, TN 37202-0801 or permissions@umpublishing.org.

This book is printed on acid-free paper.

Library of Congress Cataloging-in-Publication Data

Chakoian, Christine.
  Cryptomnesia : how a forgotten memory could save the church / Christine Chakoian.
     pages cm
  Includes bibliographical references.
  ISBN 978-1-4267-9060-7 (binding: soft back / trade pbk. : alk. paper) 1. Globalization—Religious
aspects—Christianity. 2. Christianity and culture. I. Title.
  BR115.G58C43 2014
  270.8'3—dc23

                                                                                          2014020761

Scripture quotations unless noted otherwise are from the Common English Bible. Copyright © 2011 by
the Common English Bible. All rights reserved. Used by permission. www.CommonEnglishBible.com.

Scripture quotations marked (NRSV) are taken from New Revised Standard Version of the Bible, copyright 1989, Division of Christian Education of the National Council of the Churches of Christ in the
United States of America. Used by permission. All rights reserved.

14 15 16 17 18 19 20 21 22 23—10 9 8 7 6 5 4 3 2 1
MANUFACTURED IN THE UNITED STATES OF AMERICA

To John, Annie, Karen, and Lora,
who help me remember what really matters.

Contents

Acknowledgments

The cloud of witnesses" is how the writer of Hebrews described them: the vast company of faithful people who have gone before us with courage and strength. As I consider the challenges of our time, I stand in awe of those who have struggled in faith and left their imprint of courage on us all.

And then there is the "cloud of witnesses" with me now in flesh and blood. I owe a debt of gratitude to Constance Stella, my wise and encouraging editor, and Kelsey Spinnato. Thanks to Paul Franklyn and David Teel for their grace of inviting me to participate in the Covenant Bible Study project and to cohost Shane Stanford, whose humility, faith, and courage are astonishing.

A huge thanks to my college and seminary professors who inspired the love of history and biblical studies in me, especially Vernon K. Robbins and Gary Porton, and to the Moveable Feast preaching colloquium, who keeps that love alive.

Thanks to the members of First Presbyterian Church of Lake Forest, who may never understand my nerdy scholarship but love me anyway.

Last but not least, thanks to John, Annie, Karen, and Lora, without whose encouragement I would never imagine that I had something worth saying.

Introduction

Cryptomnesia

Cryptomnesia: crypto ("hidden" or "secret") + mnesia ("memory") = the reappearance of a suppressed or forgotten memory which is mistaken for a new experience.

—*The Collins English Dictionary*

We have all had that feeling: we have seen or heard something before but we cannot quite place it. A person looks like someone we know; a song sounds familiar. But then we discover it is just déjà vu: what we are experiencing is brand new. Our brains are tricking us into thinking we have been here before.

Cryptomnesia is the opposite experience: our brains trick us into thinking we're encountering something new, when in reality we've been here before. We forget that we've witnessed or heard something, and then, later, we think it's brand new. Individuals can experience cryptomnesia—for example, when we think we have an original idea, but we've actually forgotten something we read or saw earlier. Psychologists tell us that cryptomnesia happens when students accidentally plagiarize with no awareness that they're doing it. They think their idea is original when, in fact, they are recalling a source they read or an idea generated in a discussion.

Groups can experience cryptomnesia too. Families might find themselves challenged by alcoholism or financial ruin and forget that their parents and grandparents faced the same stress. Family systems theory reminds us that forgotten patterns reemerge over and over again across generations. Similarly, congregations can fall apart over their leaders' bad behavior, squabbles over money, or tensions over worship styles—and it never occurs to them that their predecessors dealt with exactly the same issues. I discovered this phenomenon as I researched the history of my 150-year-old congregation: the same challenges replayed over multiple pastorates. Sadly, no one remembered, so each generation felt alone in the struggle.

Cryptomnesia—forgotten memory—is exactly what we're manifesting in the larger Christian community today. The twenty-first-century church is undergoing a crisis. Traditional faith practices are losing traction. Once-solid denominations are under pressure to survive. Alternative religions and secularism are pressing at the edges. Americans are rapidly becoming more worldly, mobile, and materialistic, and it feels like the church we once knew is being left behind. Growing numbers of "spiritual but not religious" people show disinterest in church, and mainline churches fear imminent demise.[1]

And all the while, the world around is shifting at a staggering rate. The digital revolution rapidly accelerated what nineteenth- and twentieth-century telegraphs and rail, telephones and airlines began: bringing diverse people and faiths together in astonishing ways. It all feels new and unsettling.

But it isn't new at all. Though Christians have never experienced this exact change before, the truth is that we've been through an uncannily similar crisis. In fact, the early church emerged in an age weirdly analogous to ours.

Just as the Internet is presently linking far-flung people, the ancient world found itself connected by a new engineering marvel: the massive Roman road-building enterprise. By the time of Christ, Roman roads traversed three continents, connecting people with unprecedented access.

Like our world today, Roman citizens were bombarded with new cultures, new commerce, new foods, and new ideas, as well as new philosophies, cults, and religions. Theirs was an era of massive disorientation, and at the same time, it was exactly the right environment for Christianity to emerge and thrive.

In the pages ahead, we will look at the challenges the earliest Christians faced and the rich possibilities they encountered. As we do, we will find ourselves on oddly familiar ground. We may even remember that we have been here before.

Chapter 1

When Everything Changes: Life in America Today

My friend Gail cherishes her childhood memories growing up in Washington State:

> I grew up at the foot of Mt. St. Helens. I was a child at her beautiful feet. "The Fujiyama of the West," they called her; and there were untold family trips to her forest campgrounds. My grandfather taking me for visits at Spirit Lake Lodge . . . playing with "pummy stone," the floating rocks left from some long-ago eruption . . . campfire nights at camp, gazing across the lake at the mountain's luminous shadow in the midnight.

These memories are more than pleasant recollections to Gail. They are part of her family's spiritual heritage and shaped her Christian identity:

> By the time I was in college and director of our church's summer camp, I had a spiritual relationship with that mountain. I hiked her surrounding hills, just as my daddy had in his Scouting days . . . the same trails, the same waterfalls, the same glimpses through shoreline trees. I thought of St. Helens as "my mountain."

Though Gail knew that all creation was God's gift for us to love, she was grateful that God, knowing the limits of our hearts, "Ordained for each one spot should prove / Beloved over all," in Rudyard Kipling's words.[1] Indeed, Gail thought of St. Helens as "*my* spot, my most beloved place on earth":

> Clearest in my memory after all these years is night upon summer night, when all the campers were finally in bed, sitting on a log gazing as the Orthodox gaze at the beloved face of their icons, praying . . . to God, to Jesus, to the Spirit, all somehow "iconned" in the glowing shape of that magnificent shadow in the darkness. In my memory even now, with Spirit Lake shimmering blue-green at her feet, it is still the most beloved and beautiful place on earth.[2]

Every one of us has been shaped *somewhere*. Some, like Gail, are stamped by a single place, but most of us are shaped by a landscape of relationships and experiences, traditions and institutions. Whether or not we feel uniformly positive about them, their familiarity gives us a sense of security. We know how to navigate the terrain. And we also know that disorienting feeling whenever a major event shifts the landscape of our lives for good or ill: we get married, or lose a job; a loved one dies, or we have our first child. What was once so familiar has changed dramatically, and our whole orientation needs to adapt until a new normal emerges.

But every now and then, in the course of human history, something happens that hits everyone at the same time—as if a tectonic shift is shaking the earth beneath us. The early Christians experienced this two thousand years ago, when the Roman Empire built its vast road system, connecting far-flung people with unprecedented ease. Now we're feeling it today as the Internet highway connects us all, rearranging everything we found familiar. And like any change that shifts our recognizable terrain, it is unsettling.

In the spring of 1980, Gail remembers, Mount St. Helens began to tremor and steam. She followed the story from her new home in New York. Then one night, she had a dream:

In my dream, I saw the mountain from my accustomed vantage across Spirit Lake; but instead of being graceful and snow-capped, she was low, gray, and ugly. . . . It left me wondering—until a week later, on a Sunday morning in May, when the mountain exploded: blowing out some 1200 feet of her summit and destroying everything living on and around those slopes, burying Spirit Lake and the trails I had hiked and my father before me, burying them forever under 150 feet of mud and ash.

The next day, I remember weeping inconsolably as I watched the nightly news, the first photos coming in from the blast area; until in mid-sob one particular aerial photo flashed for a split second on the screen. It was a distance panorama of the mountain itself—and what made me gasp was the shape—the exact outline I had dreamed a week before.[3]

Like the shifting plates of planet under the Cascade Range that caused Mount St. Helens to erupt in May of 1980, spewing fine coal over hundreds of miles and changing the face of the mountain—now and then, it feels as if the foundation of the earth is moving. When it does, not only we ourselves, but also everything and everyone around us shifts as well, and the earth moves, and the people tremble (Ps 99:1).

Such is the disorienting force of technology, shifting the earth beneath us. Everyone is unsettled—the whole world, and every single human institution in it. The result is a social volcano that transforms our landscape, leaving a new reality in its path. What was once so familiar has changed dramatically, and our whole orientation has to adapt until a new normal emerges.

Half a century ago, it wasn't a geologist but a communications professor who saw proverbial steam rising from the volcano of technology. On May 18, 1960, CBS news reporter Alan Millar introduced a professor at the University of Toronto: Marshall McLuhan, who was studying the effect of mass media on behavior and thought:

> Television has transformed the world into an interconnected tribe he calls a "global village." There's an earthquake and no matter where we live, we all get the message. And today's teenager, the future villager, who feels especially at home with our new gadgets . . . will bring our tribe even closer together.

The world has gotten smaller fast, thanks to all our "gadgets." Now every place on the planet feels like our own neighborhood:

> We know what it's like to go on a safari in Kenya or to have an audience with the pope . . . But not only is the world getting smaller. It's becoming more available and familiar, to our minds and to our emotions. The world is now a global village.[4]

Later McLuhan wrote: "So rapidly have we begun to feel the effects of the electronic revolution in presenting us with new configurations that all of us today are displaced persons living in a world that has little to do with the one in which we grew up."[5] He prophetically called ours "the Age of Anxiety."[6] And that was before the Internet exponentially accelerated the pace of change. In *The New Digital Age: Reshaping the Future of People, Nations and Business*, Eric Schmidt and Jared Cohen sum it up this way: as the reach of the Internet expands, "nearly every aspect of life will change, from the minutiae of our daily lives to more fundamental questions about identity, relationships and even our security."[7]

The early Christians who experienced the unsettling impact of Roman roads knew this kind of upheaval, and in the chapters ahead, we'll learn from them. But let's start by looking at the broad scope of disorienting change that we're experiencing now.

Technology's Impact on Daily Life

I remember growing up in a quiet suburban home using a rotary dial telephone, listening to songs on a stereo record player, and watching color television for the first time. Then, when I was in grade school, my class took the train downtown to Chicago to see an amazing new invention: the computer. It filled an entire room.

Fast-forward to today. Schmidt and Cohen describe today's breakneck advances in technology:

> Hundreds of millions of people are, each minute, creating and consuming an untold amount of digital content in an online world. . . . Think of all the websites you've ever visited, all the e-mails you've sent and stories you've read online, all the facts you've learned and fictions you've encountered and debunked. Think of every relationship forged, every journey planned, every job found and every dream born, nurtured and implemented through this platform. . . . This is the Internet, the world's largest ungoverned space.[8]

Because we're immersed in it every day, it's easy to forget the before-and-after impact of the Internet on our lives. Pause for a moment to consider how many people who are alive today remember:

- storing photographs in boxes, addresses in books, and files in folders instead of digitally archiving them online;

- writing on a typewriter instead of using spell-check corrections and cut-and-paste edits on a computer;

- going to a teller at the local bank to take out cash instead of putting a card into an ATM machine or getting change at the store; or

- researching in libraries instead of running Google searches.

And then there is the impact on our closest relationships. When my Armenian grandmother came to the United States from Turkey in 1910, she knew that she would never see her aunts and uncles and cousins again. A century later, when our daughter went to South Korea for a year to serve in mission work, we trusted that we would see her every week as we caught up over Skype.

Technology's Impact on Institutions

Technology is changing more than just our personal lives. It is impacting every institution that contributes to American culture.

Think about how the business world is being pressed to adapt. No field is exempt—from corporate headquarters to hospitals, colleges to cafeterias.

Retailers are feeling the heat. The suburb where I now live is home to the first shopping mall ever built in America: Market Square, constructed in 1914. It sits right across from the train station, so people going to or from work could stop by the store and pick something up. That was a radical idea at the time, but over the years, clusters of shops in strip malls and indoor malls popped up all over America. Then in the 1960s and '70s, big-box stores like Walmart and Target, Barnes and Noble, and Toys"R"Us began to catch on. Local businesses were overwhelmed by the large chains' competitive prices and expansive stock. Then came the Internet and e-retailers like Amazon.com, Alibaba, and eBay.

The entertainment industry is working to keep up too. In 1960, television viewers had three channels from which to choose. In 1992, Bruce Springsteen released the hit single "57 Channels (And Nothin' On)." A little more than twenty years later, cable and satellite TV now provide hundreds of stations, and viewers can pull up virtually any show on demand. Only time-sensitive programs like sporting events and awards shows require real-time viewing. The music industry is shifting too. Radio stations are being replaced by listener-directed options. *Time*'s Victor Luckerson reports a huge new competitor in the burgeoning field of music streaming:

Tech giant Samsung just rolled out an Internet radio service called Milk Music exclusively for owners of the company's Galaxy line of mobile devices. The new music service, which is powered by the Internet radio platform Slacker Radio, boasts 13 million songs and 200 different radio stations. Listeners can customize a station to suit their own taste based not on categories such as genre, overall popularity, and currentness. . . . Milk Music will compete with industry leader Pandora Radio, which has more than 75 million monthly listeners, and Apple's newly launched iTunes Radio, which had attracted about 20 million listeners.[9]

The corporate and manufacturing sector has had to adapt. Alan May, a senior executive whose career has included roles at three major global corporations, offers this perspective:

As I started my career in the early '80s, the "global" perspective of most business leaders was limited to accessing raw materials abroad, exporting finished goods to new markets, or manufacturing offshore to capture the perceived value of lower wages. Over the course of three decades, globalization has advanced in a quantum leap.

Products are often designed by employees in locations throughout the world, with components sourced in dozens of nations, then assembled in yet another location for eventual delivery to world markets. Just look at any automobile, computer, or home appliance. There is no such thing as "domestic content" in a globally interdependent supply chain of designers, producers and distributors.

Talent itself is now increasingly global, with companies tapping into "human capital" pools across the world. Look at Chinese manufacturers as they focus on making advanced products that require legions of highly educated workers; even the former "low wage" havens are now pressured by even lower wages in southeast Asia and Africa.

The fuel for expanding globalization will continue to be the availability of information enabled by the Internet. Instantaneous news, data, and social interaction has largely eliminated national boundaries and placed an entire generation on a global platform.[10]

Educational institutions are also making adaptive shifts. For years, *U.S. News and World Report* has ranked colleges and universities. Recently it added a rating system for online education. This year the top two online bachelor's degree programs are Central Michigan University and the State University of New York College of Technology in Delhi. I had to look to see if it was Delhi, India, or Delhi, New York (it's the latter). Tied for third place are Pace University in New York, and Pennsylvania State University—World Campus.[11] Just as missionaries went abroad a century ago to bring schools to the farthest reaches, now the Internet is making American higher education accessible to people around the globe.

Governments and nonprofits are changing too. For generations, well-established organizations like the Red Cross and the YMCA have helped unreached people deal with natural disasters, climb out of war, receive health care, and get an education. But now technology has enabled millions of *individuals* across the world to link together for common causes. Strangers who are passionate about an issue—whether saving the whales or funding cancer research—aren't waiting for an authority to do something. We've seen overseas movements like the Arab Spring and girls' education in Afghanistan and local causes like the Tea Party movement and those who press for gay marriage. The Internet will continue to equip people to join hands with like-minded strangers. According to Harvard's Corporate Social Responsibility Initiative, the past two decades have brought an explosion "in the number, diversity, reach and influence of civil society organizations and networks"— all "supported by unprecedented communications capacity via the Internet and global media."[12]

As global connections continue their rapid advance, no one is spared from their reach. Schmidt and Cohen warn:

Many old institutions and hierarchies will have to adapt or risk becoming obsolete, irrelevant to modern society. The struggles we see today in many businesses, large and small, are examples of the dramatic shift for society that

8

lies ahead. Communication technologies will continue to change our institutions from within and without.[13]

The question for church leaders isn't whether we need to adapt. The question is: Why should we expect religious institutions to be exempt?

Technology's Impact on the Church

Since 312 CE, when Emperor Constantine converted to Christianity, the church has played a leading role in Western society. But in recent years, the authority of the church has waned. Scholars have variously called this a post-Constantinian, postdenominational, postmodern, or even post-Christian age. What happened?

It's not that Christians are in the minority in America now—far from it. But the landscape around us has changed dramatically. For example, our society doesn't give points for—or even expect—churchgoing the way it used to. Not long ago, young families could be counted on to bring their children to Sunday school every week. Now in many parts of the country, it's entirely optional. Once, up-and-coming professionals were expected to list their leadership at church on their resume. Now it's considered a private matter.

This trend has been edging up as Americans have become increasingly individualistic in their spiritual practices. It shouldn't surprise us. For the first time, we have a generation free to choose entertainment from over five hundred television channels, unlimited YouTube videos, or movies on demand; a generation that can learn from traditional schools, online classes, or an amalgam; a generation that might shop at the corner store, the mall, or e-retailers; a generation that can choose whether to visit with friends in person, on Facebook, over Skype, or by text, phone, or e-mail. It's no wonder we're approaching faith in our own individual way too.

Robert Bellah first put a name to this tendency toward religious privatism in his 1986 lecture "Habits of the Heart." He called it "Sheilaism," based on a real woman to whom he gave the pseudonym Sheila Larson. Sheila is a young nurse who describes her faith this way: "I believe in God," Sheila says.

> "I am not a religious fanatic. I can't remember the last time I went to church. My faith has carried me a long way. It's Sheilaism. Just my own little voice." Sheila's faith has some tenets beyond belief in God, though not many. In defining "my own Sheilaism," she said: "It's just try to love yourself and be gentle with yourself. You know, I guess, take care of each other. I think He would want us to take care of each other."[14]

Sheila is hardly alone in defining faith her own particular way. Over the years, especially in places like the Pacific Northwest and New England, belonging to a church community and attending Sunday worship stopped being the cultural norm and people started to do their own thing.

Now individualism is the fastest-growing expression of spirituality. "'Nones' on the Rise" is how the Pew Research Center dubbed the eruption of the number of Americans who claim no identification with a religion:

> One-fifth of the U.S. public—and a third of adults under 30—are religiously unaffiliated today, the highest percentages ever in Pew Research Center polling. . . . This large and growing group of Americans is less religious than the public at large on many conventional measures, including frequency of attendance at religious services and the degree of importance they attach to religion in their lives.[15]

John Vest, a young colleague of mine in Chicago, sees this shift at work in his generation. In his late thirties, he's sizing up the Sunday "competition" in terms not of other successful churches but of the smorgasbord of secular alternatives. He doesn't remember a time when stores, movie theaters, and country clubs weren't open on the Sabbath. But he's seen intramural sports practices and games added to friends' Sunday morning schedules, along with school open houses, concerts and plays, birthday parties, and fund-raising runs. So at the urging of a friend to check out "rival" options, John took a

Sunday morning off to sleep in, read the paper, and watch cable news shows. Later that morning he and his wife took their two little boys for a leisurely brunch and then walked over to a local park. He says, "It was filled with families just like us—way more families than you will find in most American churches on Sunday morning."[16]

The numbers bear this out. In the last fifty years, every major mainline Protestant denomination has seen a steady slide in membership:[17]

Denomination	1960	2010	Percent Decline
United Methodist Church	10,798,000	7,679,850	28.9 percent
Evangelical Lutheran Church in America	5,300,000	4,274,855	19.3 percent
Presbyterian Church USA	4,108,000	2,675,873	34.8 percent
Episcopal Church	3,444,000	1,951,907	43.3 percent
United Church of Christ	2,022,000	1,058,423	47.6 percent
American Baptist Church	1,521,000	1,308,054	14.0 percent

This is a massive change in just fifty years. We've lost so much ground that it's hard to recognize the church that once existed. It confirms what we've seen with our own eyes: sanctuaries built to seat five hundred now see only fifty people in worship on Sunday—most of them gray-haired.

For people who care about the church, this is disturbing news. The church that raised me was a wonderful place. Our family went every week without fail. Dad was an elder and taught adult Bible study; Mom was a deacon and taught children's Sunday school. It was a thriving suburban congregation, and I'm grateful for all the ways it shaped my faith. But it's not the church that it once was.

Maybe you've had that kind of experience too. A friend of mine, Marsha Hoover, grew up in a Church of the Brethren congregation in rural Colorado where her father was the pastor. Her church shaped her faith too. The congregation has disbanded now, which breaks her heart. The Christmas after the Church of the Brethren closed its doors, Marsha wrote this poem:

The Rocky Ford Church

On Christmas Eve 1999

Every Christmas Eve I go back to Rocky Ford.
To the aching anticipation of a child on the night before Christmas.
To the gothic church on the corner of Ninth and Sycamore.

Dad has already left to go down the block.
Mom is bustling. Someone will be performing and they
Are warming up or fussing with tie or hair.
Grabbing music and donning coat as they pull the door shut.

Dad will sing.
He shall feed his flock like a shepherd.
And then he shall be home all day tomorrow.
Barring death
Or some unforeseen circumstance.

We'll get to sing the good carols at last,
And our handmade advent wreath will be alight.
And afterwards, we rush away with giggles and glee
To open faraway packages and parishioner offerings.
Summer sausage and petit fours.

Leaving the brick and block church
Dark and silent. Waiting.
Waiting for Ordinary Time. Pentecost and Easter.
For the day when they would all
Lock the doors and walk away.

When all the children whose birth dates
Hung on pink and blue ribbon in the nursery,

And all of their children and parents
Had walked or been borne away for the last time.
Had followed paths out and away to return only in their memories.

Some might be quoting creeds on Sunday now.
I believe in the communion of saints.
I believe in the communion of the Sisters
Turning Brother Stauffer's beef into the Love Feast.
Construction paper and Kool Aid into Bible School.
Jello and hot dishes into fellowship.

And I believe in the life everlasting
For tall and honest grocers who walk in humor and humility
And their gentle and steady wives.
For grandmothers who tell long sad stories
And captains of industry who fill the offering plate and stand behind
    the pastor.

For Sunday school teachers,
And ladies with hankies who sing solos,
And custodians who sweep and dole out chewing gum to children,
And for organists who wear little black pom pom slippers.
For sun baked farmers whose perfect fruit can only come from the
    divine.

And I believe in the ties that bind.
That no mortal can put asunder,
The bonds that no corporate resolution can dissolve.
Of sheep that have fed together.
Of brothers and sisters.
Of the First Noel and the Last Supper.[18]

The church that Marsha grew up in is gone. There are thousands of churches with that same sad ending and many more in serious decline. How discouraging it must feel for the "Greatest Generation" who survived the

Depression and World War II and invested so much of themselves in their churches. How disorienting for all of us who grew up at a time when the church was the center of our culture and family life. The beloved place we knew is no more.

Hope for New Pathways

Yet, in the midst of our loss and grief, there is still cause for hope. Just because we're not seeing *religion* thrive in the way it once did doesn't mean that people are not *spiritually* hungry.

The same Pew Research group that tracked Americans' choice not to affiliate with a church recently reported encouraging findings:

- Among America's approximately 46 million adults who claim to be unaffiliated, many still claim to be spiritual or even religious. Researchers note that "two-thirds of them say they believe in God (68%)."

- Although more than a third of people self-describe as "spiritual" but not "religious" (37%), researchers discovered that even among them, "21% say they pray every day."

- Attitudes toward religion are positive among many religiously unaffiliated Americans; in fact, most "think that churches and other religious institutions benefit society by strengthening community bonds and aiding the poor."[19]

Just because we're not seeing the *institutional* church thrive with the same numbers it once did doesn't mean that *Christian faith* needs to be on the defensive. The individualistic upheaval propelled by technology may be undoing the church as we knew it. But the Holy Spirit may well be carving new roads for us ahead, as theologian and author Diana Butler Bass suggests:

Strange as it may seem in this time of cultural anxiety, economic near collapse, terrorist fear, political violence, environmental crisis, and partisan anger, I believe that [we are] caught up in the throes of a spiritual awakening, a period of sustained religious and political transformation during which our ways of seeing the world, understanding ourselves, and expressing faith are being, to borrow a phrase, "born again." . . .

Exponential change creates exponential fear along with exponential hope. Massive transformation creates the double-edged cultural sword of decline and renewal. Exponential change ends those things that people once assumed and trusted to be true. At the same time, upheaval opens new pathways to the future.[20]

Remember my friend Gail? The pictures she witnessed of Mount St. Helens blowing up—scarred, cratered, covered in ash—left her heart devastated. Yet those images are not the last she saw of her beloved mountain:

Over the years I have made multiple pilgrimages up the new highway, slowly getting to know a foreign landscape. I watch it day by day now on my computer, gazing on the steam and ash plume that rises from the crater, watching the ever-changing skies. I do it to keep up on the weather "at home" (even some 35 years separated from that place); but also, I think to contemplate that mystery of what she will do next—even though after the 1980 eruption she was no longer "my" mountain in the same way. The relationship is different. [Yet] it's not the mountain that's the point, of course. What the mountain helped to give me—this ineffable relationship with a Creator God—endures.[21]

The tectonic plates are shifting. There is no stopping them. And the place that we called "home"—it will never be the same. Yet it helps when we remember that this isn't the first time we've been disoriented. As Christians, we've been through massive upheaval and the dislocation that goes with rapid change before. Cryptomnesia has dulled our memories into thinking this is all new. But in fact, as the hidden memories come back to us, we will be amazed. We'll discover again what the psalmist wrote so long ago:

God is our refuge and strength,
　　a help always near in times of great trouble.
That's why we won't be afraid when the world falls apart,
　　when the mountains crumble into the center of the sea,
　　when its waters roar and rage, when the mountains shake. (Ps 46:1-3)

God was our refuge and strength before, and God is our refuge and strength still, leading us on new paths on once-familiar ground.

Chapter 2
Religious Life in the Shrinking World

When my mom was growing up in rural Missouri, all her friends attended one of the three churches in town: Evangelical and Reformed (where her family attended), Lutheran, and Roman Catholic. When I was growing up in Illinois, there was an alphabet soup of churches: American Baptist, Congregationalist, Episcopalian, Lutheran, Methodist, Presbyterian, Roman Catholic, Swedish Covenant, and more. One of my classmates was Jewish, but that's as far as diversity went.

Today, members of my church constantly encounter myriad different religious expressions:

- Every month, Jim, a young dad in my congregation, travels across the country and often around the world for his job. Last spring, Jim's work took him to Mumbai, India, for an in-depth assignment. At the end of the week, he welcomed his driver to join his friends at dinner. The chauffeur insisted he could not, but Jim pressed him until he finally consented. Only later—after a very awkward evening—did Jim discover that the Hindu caste system was behind his driver's caution. His driver, being of lower caste, was not supposed to eat with his upper-caste counterparts.

- Last Sunday at church, Steve told me about his family's recent trip to Cambodia where they had a meeting with a Buddhist monk. It was fascinating, he said, though their legs got cramped sitting in lotus position for two hours. But I quickly was reminded that you don't have to go to Cambodia in order to discover Buddhism. That same morning, my friend Laurie asked me if I wanted to join the wonderful yoga class she attended. It was great for stretching, which is why she went; but she found it spiritually refreshing too.

- Elizabeth, who's been battling leukemia, has found that pastoral counseling and a small-group Bible study has helped with her anxiety. But she's also sought help from Reiki treatment. She tells me that the name comes from two Japanese words: *Rei*, which means "God's wisdom, or the higher power"; and *Ki*, which means "life force energy."

The truth is that, if they wanted to, everyone in our congregation could find *endless* spiritual options within reach in the Chicago suburbs. You can find Christian worship led by classically trained organists, hip-hop artists, bluegrass musicians, and contemporary praise bands; congregations that host support groups like 12-step and divorce recovery programs; or tai chi and yoga classes. "Brand"-wise, one web search generated this list within the metropolitan area: Anglican, Apostolic, Assembly of God, Baptist, Bible, Brethren, Calvary Chapel, Catholic, Christian, Church of Christ, Church of God, Congregational, Episcopal, Evangelical, Foursquare, Lutheran, Mennonite, Messianic, Methodist, Nazarene, nondenominational, Orthodox, Pentecostal, Presbyterian, Reformed, Seventh-Day Adventist, and other.[1] Roman Catholic practices alone include Benedictine, Carmelite, Franciscan, Jesuit, and more.

That's just within the Christian family. In metropolitan Chicago, we also have Jewish synagogues of every stripe and Muslim mosques and Islamic centers. We have Jain, Sikh, Buddhist, and Baha'i temples. We have theosophical societies, a Bodhi spiritual center, transcendental meditation clubs, and an "atheist church."[2] We have psychics who will predict your future by studying

18

the palm of your hand or the bottom of your feet, your tea leaves or coffee grounds, a crystal ball or how the stars align.

How does anyone navigate this vast maze of spiritual options? There is no map in our glove box, no map on our iPhone.

And yet it's amazing how much the post-Constantinian/postdenominational/postmodern/post-Christian church has in common with the pre-Constantinian/predenominational/premodern/pre-Christian terrain. Cryptomnesia has just caused us to forget that this isn't the first time we've experienced what Marshall McLuhan called "the global village." We have been here before.

The Ancient "Global Village"

We can only imagine what life was like for those who lived in antiquity, when their universe was only as large as the space they could travel on foot. Aside from military expeditions and the most intrepid traders, most people spent their entire lives within a few square miles, out of touch with anyone outside their tribe.

What created the first-century "global village"? It started when the Egyptians, Phoenicians, and Greeks mastered the sea, linking cultures through trade networks across the Mediterranean.³ The world shrank more in the fourth century BCE, when Alexander the Great united Greece and conquered territories from India to Africa.

Then, in 27 BCE, Augustus came to power, ushering in the Roman Empire. (Caesar—or Emperor—Augustus is the one behind the tax registration around the time of Jesus's birth [Luke 2:1].) Augustus's reign began two centuries of relative peace, known as the *Pax Romana*. Under his watch, the Empire expanded to the western edge of Africa and Europe. To the east, the peace he secured with the Parthian Empire opened trade across Asia.

Yet something bigger still was about to happen: the Empire's massive road-building project. The lives of ordinary citizens would never be the same.

While other cultures—including the Egyptians and the Persians—had developed paving, Rome made it an engineering art form. By the time of the birth of Christ, "the people of the Roman Empire traveled more extensively and more easily than had anyone before them—or would again until the nineteenth century," reports historian Wayne Meeks.⁴ So secure was the engineering that two thousand years later, some Roman roads still survive.

Eventually fifty thousand miles of paving radiated from the Forum in Rome, inspiring the statement "All roads lead to Rome." Although much of the travel on these routes was for the military and imperial administration, countless individuals took advantage of them too, for commerce, education, and even vacations.⁵ At the same time, the Chinese Han Empire had its own "Silk Road"—a caravan route through the Parthian and Kushite Empires (now Afghanistan, Pakistan, and India). People were connected from the Pacific to the Atlantic coasts.

Can you imagine the overwhelming change, novelty, and excitement? Trade routes thrived, bringing exotic lacquerware and silk from China, pearls and ivory from India, spices and precious stones from Arabia, gold and incense from East Africa, olive oil and wine from southern Europe, and silver and tin from Spain.

But it wasn't just commerce that crossed the ancient empires. People had never been exposed to such varied cultures, languages, traditions, foods, or religions. Says Meeks, "It is not surprising that the spread of foreign cults closely followed the spread of trade."[6] Imagine this scene in Ostia—the harbor city of ancient Rome—where ordinary citizens lived:

> In addition to houses, offices, workshops, and laundries, the city boasted an
> astonishing array of religious buildings. . . . Side-by-side with temples to the
> gods of the Greco-Roman pantheon and the imperial cults stand Christian
> baptisteries, a Jewish synagogue, and a host of temples to Near Eastern dei-
> ties, including a dozen dedicated to the Zoroastrian divinity Mithras, the god
> of contracts and thus revered by merchants.[7]

So interconnected was the Roman Empire with surrounding regions that by the third century CE, Diogenes Laertius's *Lives of Eminent Philosophers* included reference to the Persians' Zoroastrian Magi, the Indians' Gymnoso-phists, and the Celts' and Gauls' Druids and Holy Ones, as well as Egyptian, Libyan, and Phoenician gods.[8] For some people this open-endedness was just the breath of fresh air they needed. But for others, it was a disorienting ca-cophony of spiritual options.

Varieties of Spiritual Options

It is impossible to do justice to the dizzying array of religious choices available to ordinary people in the Roman Empire. What follows is just a sampling of the diverse spirituality practiced in the era of the early church.

Philosophies

By the time of Jesus, it had been some centuries since high Greek phi-losophy had reigned supreme. Yet the school of thought taught by Socrates (469–399 BCE) and expanded by his student Plato (427–347 BCE) at the

Academy in Athens continued to influence the world across the Roman Empire. The philosophers' major contribution was the rigorous pursuit of wisdom: How does one live well?[9]

Neoplatonists: Plato was known for his dualistic contrast of the corrupt physical world and the ideal world. Plutarch (ca. 45–120 CE) is among those who continued Plato's teaching. Best remembered for his biography of Greek and Roman leaders (*Parallel Lives*), Plutarch also wrote essays reflecting a dualistic approach to life: when the soul was concerned with the body, it led to disorder and vice; when the soul attended to intellect instead, it promoted virtue, order, and benevolence.[10]

Gnostics: This school of thought takes its name from the Greek word for "insight" (the same root for the English word *knowledge*). Like the Neoplatonists, Gnostics embraced dualism: the world as we know it is prone to evil; only the disembodied world of the soul is able to be good. Gnosticism was found not only in Hellenistic circles (e.g., in *Corpus Hermeticum*) but also in Jewish and Christian writing.[11] The library at Nag Hammadi, excavated in 1945, brought to light many of these texts.

Stoics: Ethical living—with justice, moderation, and courage—was the focus of the Stoics' concern. Stoicism is named after the *stoa*, or porch, at the Agora in Athens where philosophers met to debate. (This was where Paul argued with both Stoics and Epicureans in Acts 17:18.) Stoics believed that virtue and calm were the highest good, while passion and emotions were dangerous distractions to be controlled.[12] Their idea of detachment from striving is not unlike Buddhist teaching. Prominent writers included Seneca (1 BCE–65 CE, born in Cordoba [Spain] and educated in Rome)[13] and Epictetus (55 CE–ca. 135 CE, born a slave in Hierapolis, Asia Minor).[14]

Epicureans: Our modern equation of "epicureanism" with hedonism can obscure its ancient focus. This philosophy takes its name from Epicurus (341–271 BCE), who advocated appreciation of the real world and pleasure as a worthy goal. Epicureans in the first century CE were pragmatic and utilitarian, realists rather than idealists. Yet, like the Stoics, happiness for Epicureans was equated not with striving but with tranquility.[15]

Cults and Mystery Religions

The pantheon of gods: In both ancient Greek and Roman myth, each aspect of nature had its own god. By the time of the Empire, syncretism had virtually merged the two systems. The Greek/Roman equivalents included:

- Zeus/Jupiter, god of sky and air and chief among gods;

- Hera/Juno, goddess of home and family;

- Demeter/Ceres, goddess of the harvest;

- Poseidon/Neptune, god of the sea; and

- Ares/Mars, god of war.

Family rituals, civic events, festival days, sacrifices, and processions celebrated the beneficence of the gods. The enduring importance of the gods is reflected in the building of the Pantheon in Rome by Marcus Agrippa in 27 BCE and, after fires in 80 and 110 CE, its renovation. It stands to this day.

The imperial cult: One way to unite the highly diverse Empire was through the imperial cult: worship and honors afforded to the emperor. Since the traditional Roman religion would shrink from calling a living human divine, the first emperor, Augustus (63 BCE–14 CE), was known as "son of god." (It was less of a concern in Egyptian and Greek cultures.) But by the time of Caligula (37–41 CE), Nero (54–68 CE), and Domitian (81–96 CE), deification was awarded to living emperors.[16] The aim of the imperial cult was largely political; nevertheless, it created difficulty for some sects, including Jews and Christians. This is the concern behind the Pharisees' question to Jesus in Matthew 22:17: "Is it lawful to pay taxes to the emperor, or not?" (NRSV).

Mystery religions: For centuries in ancient Greece, mystery cults thrived. Initiates were inducted into the cult through secret education and rituals. Among the best-known cults were the Dionysian mysteries, which were associated with bacchanalia, and the Eleusinian mysteries, which were more akin to civic religion.

As the Empire grew, exotic foreign mysteries grew increasingly attractive. The popularity of the Egyptian mysteries of Isis, for example, is evident in temples and inscriptions in Rome and Athens, at the Arabian and Black Seas, and as far west as Britain, Gaul, and Spain.[17] The Persian-Indian cult of Mithras was adapted from Zoroastrianism and transformed as it was carried by the Roman military; it was considered among the steepest competition to emerging Christianity.[18]

Magic, astrology, and divination: The magical worldview of the ancient world is chronicled in scripture. It included astrology, such as the belief of the magi who followed the star to Bethlehem (Matt 2:1). It also involved fortune-telling (cf. Acts 16:16); at places like Delphi in Greece, divination was offered by an oracle (priestess) who made predictions of the future. Charms, spells, and incantations were also common (cf. Acts 8:9 and following), whether offered positively by healers and miracle workers or negatively by those who cursed in the name of demons.[19]

It seems that Jews were among those who were attracted to these various options. The writer Philo (20 BCE–50 CE) offered this scathing warning against the lure of the mysteries and rites:

> He banishes from the sacred legislation the lore of occult rites and mysteries and all such imposture and buffoonery. He would not have those who were bred in such a commonwealth as ours take part in mummeries and clinging on to mystic fables despite the truth and pursue things which have taken

night and darkness for their province, discarding what is fit to bear the light of day. Let none, therefore, of the followers and disciples of Moses either confer or receive initiation to such rites. For both in teacher and taught such action is gross sacrilege. For tell me, ye mystics, if these things are good and profitable, why do you shut yourselves up in profound darkness and reserve their benefits for three or four alone, when by producing them in the midst of the market-place you might extend them to every man and thus enable all to share in security a better and happier life?[20]

Options in Judaism

What an array of gods and philosophies, lifestyles and practices were suddenly available to the average citizen! Not surprisingly, some people found it utterly overwhelming. They longed to protect their traditional worship and protect what was familiar, comforting, and true. Others were thrilled to explore the possibilities and gladly embraced the freedom, excitement, and novelty. Still others chose to adapt, preserving some of the old but also trying on some new practices for size. This was true for the Jews both within Jerusalem and in the Diaspora across the Empire. What would it mean to be a faithful Jew in this new reality? There were myriad answers.

The Temple: Since the time of King Solomon (tenth century BCE), the Temple in Jerusalem was the center of the worship of Yahweh. Though it was destroyed by the Babylonians in 586 BCE, it was rebuilt by King Cyrus of Persia (516 BCE; cf. Ezra–Nehemiah). In 20 BCE, King Herod set about reconstructing the Temple to an even grander scale.

Many faithful Jews from across the Empire undertook pilgrimages to the Temple in Jerusalem: for Rosh Hashanah, Yom Kippur, and Succoth in the fall; Hanukkah in the winter; and Passover and Pentecost in the spring. In addition, daily sacrifices, rituals, purifications, and prayers were held year-round. The Temple staff included the Zadokite priests and the Levites.[21]

Synagogues: While the Temple remained the official cultic center, for ordinary Jews in Judea and the Diaspora, the local synagogue was home for regular worship. A liturgy developed with common prayer, and the Law and the Prophets were regularly read.[22] Depending on its location, the language of the synagogue was more often Greek or Aramaic than Hebrew. When scripture was read, it was likely the Septuagint: the Greek translation of the Hebrew Bible created in the third to second centuries BCE.

The Sanhedrin: The Roman Empire allowed for local jurisdiction in many matters of the daily life of its citizens. For the Jews, this authority was based in the Sanhedrin—the religious court and legislature based in Jerusalem. There are some differences in the way ancient writers describe it. The Talmud—written by rabbis and finalized after the fall of the Temple in 70 CE—included a tractate on the Sanhedrin that painted it as primarily a religious body.[23] The Jerusalem-based historian Josephus (37–100 CE) described it as a council that included civic responsibilities. Its political duties included appointing the king and even declaring war. Likely controlled by the Sadducees, its membership included Pharisees as well and was headed by the high priest.[24]

Sadducees: The Sadducees composed the aristocracy of Judaism. Just as aristocrats today can be born into it or come into it through wealth, Sadducees "either descended from high priestly families or more recently connected with the temple hierarchy through their wealth," writes scholar Julie Galambush. "Members of the wealthy upper class, the Sadducees tended to support Roman rule. They were religiously conservative, accepting no beliefs (in particular, the belief in a resurrection) that did not appear in the Torah."[25] Among their beliefs was a confidence in free will, as historian Josephus noted: "They maintain that man has the free choice of good or evil, and that it rests with each man's will whether he follows the one or the other."[26]

Pharisees: Like our modern class system, the Pharisees were one rung below the Sadducees. Well-educated, they were likely members of merchant and landholding classes. They were also scrupulous in their interpretation of the law. Their commitment to the letter of the law separated them from the wider culture. (Galambush notes that the name "Pharisee" is linked to the Hebrew *parush*, which means "separate.")

But unlike the Sadducees, they also followed the "Oral Torah"—teachings of the elders handed down from generation to generation that expanded the Hebrew Bible. These teachings included, for example, belief in divine intervention and belief in the resurrection. As Josephus wrote: "They attribute everything to Fate, and to God; they hold that to act rightly or otherwise rests, indeed, for the most part with men, but that in each action Fate cooperates. Every soul, they maintain, is imperishable, but the soul of the good alone passes into another body, while the souls of the wicked suffer eternal punishment."[27] Their teachings had an indelible impact on modern Judaism. Following the destruction of the Temple in 70 CE, the Oral Torah was transposed into the Mishnah and Talmud, eventually giving rise to rabbinic Judaism.[28]

Essenes: In modern times we've come to know the Essenes through the Dead Sea Scrolls of the Qumran community. The Essenes were religious purists, separating themselves from the larger community much as later Christian desert monastics would. Included in their ritual was a water bath called the *mikvah* in which followers immersed themselves for sacred cleansing. Josephus wrote, "They shun pleasures as a vice and regard temperance and the control of passions as a special virtue. . . . Riches they despise, and their community of goods is truly admirable; you will not find one among them distinguished by greater opulence than another."[29] Admission was strict, and induction took two years of preparation.[30]

The Essenes fervently embraced the messianic hopes of the time and welcomed the expected apocalypse. Galambush places their separatism from society as preparation "for the upcoming climax in the struggle between good and evil. Such groups saw themselves—separated, purified, and prepared to live or die with the coming messiah—as the only 'true' Israel, the lonely remnant who stood firm while others were corrupted by wickedness." John the Baptist and his followers may well have been an Essene community.[31]

Zealots: The Zealots were less an organized group than a movement: revolutionaries who desired more than anything to overthrow the power of Rome and reinstate Jewish purity and independence. Zealots emerged with regularity throughout the Roman occupation, inciting riots and rebellions and undercutting those Jews who went along with Roman rule.[32]

Scribes: The work of the scribe is described in the Gospels primarily as "writer" or "copyist" (*grammateus*, Mark and Matthew). Most of their duties involved official inscription; for example, producing legal documents, recording deeds, copying scriptures, and so on. At a time when papyri and parchment were used across the Empire, the educated scribe was in high demand. Yet the position carried far more authority than a secretarial assistant; Luke uses the term "lawyer" (*nomikos*). At times the scribe carried the role of the teacher as well.[33]

But for all of the divisions of class, political, and religious affiliation, scholar Julie Galambush urges us to keep sight of the ordinary Jewish citizen:

> The vast majority of Judeans would have belonged to none of these distinct parties. In Judea as in the diaspora, Jews seem by and large to have continued to revere the Jerusalem temple and to pay an annual tax to support temple sacrifices. . . . [Nevertheless,] while most people were far too preoccupied with survival to embrace one of the dominant parties of the day, sympathy for one or another of them—admiration for the Pharisees' learning or for the Zealots' patriotism (or both)—must have been widespread.[34]

Moving Forward with Faith

Cryptomnesia would lead us to believe that we're the first ones who have ever been so overwhelmed with choices and change. Yet two thousand years ago, across the Roman Empire, people were exposed to just as stunning a range of religious experience, an explosion of choices that rival our own. There were competing views about what being a faithful Jew looked like and how to navigate the pressures of empire in the "global village." There were ancient practices, like the Temple, and emerging traditions like the synagogue. And there were myriad new options to sample, from learned philosophies to street magicians, from secret mystery religions to the very public imperial cult.

How did the early Christians navigate this complex new terrain? In the following pages, we'll look more closely at the four key disciplines they practiced. For now, here's a glimpse of our work ahead:

1. The early Christians did careful <u>theological sifting</u> within their community: discerning what was central—and what was not—from their inherited faith. Because God had been present in that past, it was not easy; but if they kept absolutely everything they would be worshiping the past instead of worshiping God. They sorted through values and practices in worship and everyday life. Avoiding meat offered to idols—not essential. Circumcision—amazingly enough, since it was the sign of the covenant—not essential. But Christ, and him crucified—essential. Sounds obvious to us, right? But it wasn't to them.

2. The early church also had to figure out <u>authority within community</u>: how to discern what to do and who got to decide. It wasn't always clear. The same Roman roads that brought people together also undercut hierarchy; witness Paul's radical statement that in Christ "there is neither Jew nor Greek; there is neither slave nor free; nor is there male and female" (Gal 3:28).

3. The first Christians learned how to become savvy <u>cultural interpreters</u> to the world. Paul at the Areopagus is a case in point: when he was in Athens he didn't just debate in the synagogue, he also went into the city square. And before citing his scripture he quoted their poets (Acts 17:22).

4. Last but not least, the early church had to figure out how to <u>honor each other's ministry in spite of differences.</u> Again and again, early Christians struggled to put faithfulness to the gospel ahead of their differences: differences regarding the law and grace, differences over authority, differences about moral issues like marrying nonbelievers and eating meat offered to idols. It wasn't always pretty, and they didn't always work together. Yet, rather than battle each other, they focused on differentiating themselves from rival options in the Greco-Roman mission field. As long as they kept faithful to what was central, they tried to honor each other because the good news of the gospel was essential—far more essential than their differences.

It is amazing how much we have in common with the first Christians. As we reclaim their well-honed tools, we'll learn how useful they are for our changing world today.

Chapter 3

Sifting Our Inheritance: What to Keep and What to Let Go?

A few years ago, my mom passed away. Blessedly, she died a peaceful death after having lived a good long life: married to my dad for over sixty years, they'd raised five kids, enjoyed ten grandchildren, and savored many friendships. After we gathered for a moving funeral that celebrated her life and witnessed to the resurrection, Dad asked us to help him sort through my mother's possessions.

Though we knew this task was coming, it was unexpectedly hard. Not because my mother had a lot of things—she wasn't a collector or a fashion maven—but because many things had memories associated with them: the seashells from my parents' trip to Mexico, the picture from her first grandchild's graduation, a string of pearls handed down from her mother. Of course, there were a number of things that were easy to throw out or give to charity, like her shoes and socks, pants and sweatshirts. In fact, most things weren't precious—they had been useful for her lifestyle but weren't needed any longer.

But a surprising number of her possessions required thought and prompted conversation among her children. What worth did each item have—not just in financial terms but also in the story it told, the values it reflected, and the memories it carried? What did we want to make sure her grandchildren received from her to carry forward into their own lives—not just of their grandmother's things but also of her identity, her struggles, her triumphs, her hard-won wisdom? Eventually it boiled down to two categories: What was obviously so important that we needed to keep it? And what didn't matter one way or the other—if somebody wanted it, great; if not, then let it go? It felt less like a burden than a sacred privilege to make these decisions.

It strikes me that the twenty-first-century church is facing a similar responsibility. Our generation has inherited the sizable holdings of a church that thrived in its time. But as the first chapter outlined, much about that church is gone. In a great  many congregations, we no longer expect to see packed pews in worship and wall-to-wall children in Sunday school. We no longer expect that most Ameri-cans will memorize scripture or sing the classic hymns by heart. And we no longer expect to hear the church's voice of justice and morality received with authority in our culture. The particular life of the church as we knew it fifty years ago has passed on. Now it falls to the next generation to sort through what we've received.

But rather than being a burden, it's a sacred privilege to consider together what we've inherited. Because everything is packed with memories, it isn't easy. Yet we know that if we kept everything, we wouldn't be honoring our mother church's life. We'd just be building a museum.

What's required of our generation is *discernment*. What worth does each item have in the story it tells, the values it reflects, and the memories it carries? What do we want to make sure future generations receive from the church's identity, struggles, triumphs, and hard-won wisdom to carry forward into their own lives? Eventually, our work boils down to two categories: What are the precious things that are so important that we need to keep? And what are the things that once were useful but now could either be kept or let go of?

In *The Great Emergence*, Phyllis Tickle's first book about our era of change, Tickle credits Anglican bishop Mark Dyer with the idea that it's time for the church to "hold a giant rummage sale."[1] I don't think that's disrespectful; in fact, it may be the perfect image.

But how do we decide what to keep and what we can let go of? Our first step is to look back to learn how our early predecessors faced these same challenges. We are hardly the first to be required to do this work of discernment. Cryptomnesia may have clouded our memories, but in fact, this is the same sorting that many Christians in the past have had to do, beginning with the very first believers. Theologians even have technical terms (in Latin, no less) for this work of sacred housecleaning. The central items that are so obviously "keepers" are called *esse* (essential); the things that could be either retained or released are called *adiaphora* (indifferent).

As we examine some key areas that the early church had to sort out, we may be surprised at what they chose to keep and what they let go. We will also learn some important tips about how our generation can move forward discerning what's so central that it's crucial to keep, and what we might clutch less tightly, allowing for differing opinions along the way.

Sorting the Inheritance among the First Christians

Just like sorting through my mother's things, there are some precious possessions in the church's life that are so obviously essentials—"keepers"—

that everyone is in agreement. It was certainly true for the early Christians as they looked to their inheritance of worship, belief, and behavior.

Let's start with worship. For the original disciples, the Temple in Jerusalem was clearly the most sacred place on earth, as it had been for two millennia for faithful Jews. It was the only place where sacrifices to Yahweh, the one holy God, could properly be offered. The priests' incense and processions, the daily offerings and prayers, the sacrifices and purification rites, the people's pilgrimages from across the Empire for high holy days: all of these set a stake in the ground in the midst of the encroaching culture. Jesus himself approached the Temple with the highest regard, expecting even higher purity than the priests who served it did (see, e.g., Matt 21:12-17). It shouldn't surprise us that the book of Acts records that "every day, [the believers] met together in the temple" (2:46).

Yet, long before the time of Jesus, alternative forms of faithful Jewish worship had begun to develop. Why? Because more Jews in the Roman Empire lived *outside* Jerusalem than *inside* it, rendering it impossible to make Temple worship a regular practice. As a result, historian C. K. Barrett reminds us that

> the Temple and its services were, even at the great Festivals when Jerusalem was thronged with worshippers, for the few. The majority of Jews found corporate practice of their religion *in the Synagogue*, where the Law and the Prophets were read, and the community engaged in common prayer.[2]

Synagogue worship helped people keep their Jewish identity as they navigated life in a pagan world. Every week, when they came together on the Sabbath, they remembered who they were and where they came from, what really mattered, and how to behave in a way that glorified the living God. So Jesus's followers inherited worship in both the Temple and the synagogue. Indeed, all four gospels attest to Jesus himself teaching frequently in synagogues throughout the region (Matt 4:23; 9:35; 12:9; 13:54; Mark 1:21; 3:1; 6:2; Luke 4:15, 16, 44; 13:10; John 6:59; 18:20).

What were synagogues like then? Unlike the Temple, they weren't especially fancy; they weren't even constructed as houses of worship. They were simply houses. Since a fairly large home was needed to accommodate the gathering, communities often met in the more-spacious house of their wealthiest member. As time went on, a number of communities set aside houses exclusively for religious use, as archaeology at places like Duro-Europos, Stobi, and Delos suggests.

What happened when they met? Synagogue worship included scripture and interpretation (as Jesus was known to do), as well as prayers and sometimes songs. While there were no sacrifices—that practice was reserved for the Temple—a number of rites developed over time. They included ritual washing, initiation ceremonies, and common meals.[3]

So widespread and vibrant was the life of the synagogue that even when the Temple in Jerusalem was destroyed by imperial forces in 70 CE, both Judaism and Christianity emerged with a vital and secure way forward. Indeed, for the first generation of Christians, much of the life of the synagogue proved to be a crucial inheritance to hand on to the next generations.

These were the beloved and familiar Jewish religious practices that the early Christians sorted through as they sought to follow Jesus's way. For a long time, Jesus's followers did not consider themselves a different religion at all. They were a Jewish sect surrounding their particular teacher, just as various rabbis and John the Baptist had their own schools. And, in fact, every school was going through the same process of sorting through the traditions they inherited. The Sadducees and Essenes, scribes and Pharisees were all discerning among themselves what was essential to keep and what could be let go of. So what did the first generations of Jesus's disciples decide?

Some things were obviously essential. First and foremost, they kept the synagogue's central focus on scripture—the Hebrew Bible, our Old Testament—which had been canonized and translated into common Greek around the second century BCE. "The Law and the Prophets" were sacred texts to them, just as they had been to Jesus. In addition, the early Christians also cherished the teachings of Jesus, recounting them much as the rabbis of their time passed along the Jewish oral tradition (the Mishnah) for instruction. This was followed by additional interpretation by local teachers. In Christian worship the interpretation was primarily instruction, as it had been in the synagogue; but it might also include songs, prophecy, and speaking in tongues. Early on, leadership was apparently shared. In his first letter to the Corinthians, Paul instructs the believers, "When you meet together, each one has a psalm, a teaching, a revelation, a tongue, or an interpretation" (1 Cor 14:26). Later, a more structured format and teaching authority emerged (see, e.g., 1 Tim 3).

In addition, Jesus's followers maintained as essential the synagogue customs of ritual baths and shared meals, but they adapted these customs in new forms. The common meal became the Lord's Supper, which took a distinctively Christian shape. In 1 Corinthians 11, Paul admonishes the church for missing the point of the common meal. They were treating it like a supper club: "So when you get together in one place, it isn't to eat the Lord's meal. Each of you goes ahead and eats a private meal. One person goes hungry while another is drunk" (1 Cor 11:20-21). Then, even though Paul was a convert who hadn't been at the table at Jesus's last supper, he knew by heart the already well-established tradition behind the Lord's Supper (1 Cor 11:23-25):

> On the night on which he was betrayed, the Lord Jesus took bread. After giving thanks, he broke it and said, "This is my body, which is for you; do this to remember me." He did the same thing with the cup, after they had eaten, saying, "This cup is the new covenant in my blood. Every time you drink it, do this to remember me."

In a similar way, the Christian practice of baptism emerged out of the synagogue's ritual cleansing ceremony. But baptism became something more than the synagogue's tradition. For the early church, baptism—rather than circumcision—also became the rite of initiation. In a moment we'll look at how that happened.

What about the precious inheritance of belief? One crucial conviction that Jesus's followers all shared was the belief in only one God, Yahweh. As we noted in the last chapter, Jewish monotheism stood in stark contrast to the surrounding culture. The Greeks, Romans, and Egyptians all had pantheons of gods. Various mystery religions' secret rites related to a range of deities. And across the Empire, the imperial cult demanded sacrifices to Caesar regardless of his subjects' worship of any other gods.

In spite of cultural pressure to believe in many gods, there was never a question for the early Christians regarding the centrality of this inheritance. It was obvious to them that they would whole-heartedly worship Yahweh alone, just as Jesus did. They strove to fulfill what Jesus called the first and most important commandment: "You must love the Lord your God with all your heart, with all your being, and with all your mind" (Matt 22:37). Unlike all the other purported gods in the Empire, Yahweh was the one who sought and kept covenant, who was "compassionate and merciful, very patient, full of great loyalty and faithfulness, showing great loyalty to a thousand generations, forgiving every kind of sin and rebellion" (Exod 34:6-7). This belief in Yahweh as God alone was a sacred inheritance, even after Paul and others started proselytizing among the pantheistic Greeks.

Finally, Jesus's followers considered many of the ethics of behavior they had inherited as essential. The goal of a righteous life was not lost on the first believers. Over and over again they turned to the second bottom line of Jesus's teaching: in addition to loving Yahweh alone as God, faith compels us to "love your neighbor as you love yourself" (Matt 22:39).

What did loving one's neighbor look like? Many of scripture's great commandments spelled it out: honoring one's mother and father (Exod 20:12); refraining from theft and covetousness, adultery and murder (Exod 20:13-17); caring for the poor (Exod 22:25-27); and reaching out to the widow and the orphan (Exod 22:22). On this, the apostles agreed. Paul corrected the Corinthians, for example, for prizing the gifts of prophecy or tongues more than love

(1 Cor 13:1-3) and for ignoring and humiliating the hungry in their midst (1 Cor 11:21-22). James especially spelled out the ethics of the Christian life:

> What good is it if people say they have faith but do nothing to show it? Claiming to have faith can't save anyone, can it? Imagine a brother or sister who is naked and never has enough food to eat. What if one of you said, "Go in peace! Stay warm! Have a nice meal!"? What good is it if you don't actually give them what their body needs? In the same way, faith is dead when it doesn't result in faithful activity. (Jas 2:13-17)

While many people in the Greco-Roman world were still searching for the meaning of life through the hedonism of pagan practices, spiritualism of mystery cults, or esoteric wisdom of philosophies, Jesus's followers knew that they had already found it. The essential gift of God's covenant was valuable beyond measure. Jesus taught them by example to embrace the traditions of the synagogue, pointing them to faithful worship. And Jesus taught them through his words and deeds how to focus on the essentials of the Law and the Prophets: loving God and loving neighbor.

Adiaphora—Indifferent Things— among the Early Believers

It's clear that the early Christians treasured their inheritance of faith. But as they moved forward, they discovered that they couldn't keep *everything* they had received. As we have seen, each Jewish sect was already wrestling with how to keep faithful as they navigated their way in a pagan world. There were disagreements between Pharisees and Sadducees, Essenes and Zealots about what was essential and what was not. Through the Jewish Talmud—the product of rabbis from different Pharisaic schools—we know that even *within* each movement there were multiple conflicting opinions.

Imagine, then, how difficult it became when the followers of Jesus felt moved to take their faith beyond Jewish circles and into *pagan* territory.

Through the movement of the Holy Spirit, they became convinced that Yahweh's covenant with Israel had been expanded to include the whole world God loved—so that the world "won't perish but will have eternal life" (John 3:16). Suddenly, they saw the covenant expanded to include *not just the Jews* but also *all who followed the way of God's Son, Jesus,* the way that leads to life.

This vastly complicated matters. Though they still agreed on essential things, such as worshiping God alone, the authority of the scriptures and Jesus's word, and the love of God and neighbor, they were now faced with the extraordinarily difficult work of determining what beliefs, behaviors, and aspects of worship were *adiaphora*—indifferent things.

Two issues proved to be particularly nettlesome. The first involved a controversy over whether it was acceptable to eat "unclean" food. The second asked whether circumcision would still be the necessary rite of initiation into the covenant.

The conundrum about unclean foods went beyond the Torah's prohibitions against *treif* (nonkosher) foods like shellfish and pork. It was possible to avoid those, much as vegetarians find a way to avoid eating meat today. A much more complicated issue arose around whether to eat food or drink wine that had been dedicated to idols. Especially in urban settings, the more intertwined the Empire became, the more frequently foods shared in social settings were dedicated as offerings to various gods before they were served.

"The celebrations of many cults were closely bound up with civic and social life since religion and politics were indivisible in ancient Hellenistic city life," scholar David Garland explains. Civic life entailed participation in sacrificial meals at festivals. Trade groups all had their own specific gods. Voluntary associations' social meals often involved some food sacrificed to an idol. Even funeral societies, which gathered to contribute to a patron's proper burial, included religious activity over a meal. Garland adds:

> Individuals might also receive invitations to a banquet at a temple since rooms could be rented out for private functions, like church halls today. Extant

papyrus invitations beckon guests to attend banquets in a temple dining room commemorating a variety of rites of passage: weddings, childbirth, birthdays, coming-of-age parties, election victories, and funerals. Others were more overtly cultic feasts celebrating, for example, a god's birthday.[4]

Jewish leaders were clear; the rabbis behind the Babylonian Talmud went to great lengths to discourage Jews from participating in this behavior, but the economic and social pressure was immense.[5] You can imagine the social and economic pressure to participate. It would be as if every present-day "sweet sixteen" party included a cake dedicated to Venus, and you have to tell your daughter that she can't attend; or as if every Rotary or Kiwanis meeting included a pledge to Mars, so you have to forgo business relationships in your community.

Among the early Christians there were differing opinions, which created a lot of controversy along the way. How did some of them decide that eating nonkosher foods or even food offered to idols was *adiaphora* (indifferent)?

It begins in Acts 10, where we learn of Peter's game-changing vision that allowed for believers to let go of prohibitions against nonkosher food: "He saw heaven opened up and something like a large linen sheet being lowered to the earth by its four corners. Inside the sheet were all kinds of four-legged animals, reptiles, and wild birds. A voice told him, 'Get up, Peter! Kill and eat!'" (Acts 10:11-13). Peter protested that the food was impure and unclean (i.e., not kosher). But the voice responded: "Never consider unclean what God has made pure" (10:14-16).

But one person's vision was not enough to change the whole church, especially on an issue this central to Jewish faith and practice. Peter's revelation had to be *discerned in community*. Thus, Peter's vision was confirmed only when he shared his vision with the believers in Jerusalem and they engaged in holy conversation (Acts 11:1-10). In the end, the Jerusalem Council stopped short of giving permission to eat food offered to idols. In Acts 15:22-31, the apostles and elders sent a letter to Gentile believers confirming a number of things as essential, including avoiding food offered to idols (Acts 15:29). Their instruction could not have been clearer.

Yet even that ruling was challenged as the holy conversation continued. We see it in the writings of Paul, who taught that food offered to idols was *adiaphora* (indifferent), since the "god" to whom it was offered wasn't real. As Paul wrote to believers in Corinth:

> Hence, as to the eating of food offered to idols, we know that "no idol in the world really exists," and that "there is no God but one." Indeed, even though there may be so-called gods in heaven or on earth—as in fact there are many gods and many lords—yet for us there is one God, the Father, from whom are all things and for whom we exist, and one Lord, Jesus Christ, through whom are all things and through whom we exist. (1 Cor 8:4-6 NRSV)

The only objection Paul had concerned the impact the behavior might have on someone else whose faith wasn't as strong. Out of concern for the weak, Paul urged awareness, compassion, and accommodation toward those with a more conservative view:

> Since some have become so accustomed to idols until now, they still think of the food they eat as food offered to an idol; and their conscience, being weak, is defiled. . . . [So] if others see you, who possess knowledge, eating in the temple of an idol, might they not, since their conscience is weak, be encouraged to eat food sacrificed to idols? (1 Cor 8:7, 10 NRSV)

Over time, Jewish food laws regarding both *treif* (nonkosher) and food offered to idols no longer troubled most Christians. Especially for those living outside Jerusalem, they accommodated the Greco-Roman culture and participated in the larger society's meals with a clear conscience.

But the dismissal of another Jewish law proved far more incendiary: the rite of circumcision for men. Since God's initial covenant with Abraham, circumcision had been *the* mark of the covenant with the Jews for millennia. Moreover, though numerous pagans were attracted to Judaism, few of them were willing to become full initiates through circumcision. Instead, many participated at the edges of the community as "God-fearers"—converts in everything but this crucial ritual of initiation into the covenant.

Because Jesus and his first disciples were faithful Jews who sought to worship the one true God, it was assumed that converts who followed him would be circumcised too, at least if they wanted to be full members of the covenant community. After all, Jesus had called them to fulfill all righteousness. It is hard to overstate how controversial it was for circumcision to be seen as *adiaphora*, indifferent. To be a faithful and righteous member of the covenant, circumcision was *esse*, essential!

So what happened among the early Christians that turned circumcision from an absolutely essential part of the tradition to keep and made it something that people could agree to disagree about? Again, both the book of Acts and Paul's letters give a glimpse of the community's discernment that changed the course of history.

For the first part of the book of Acts, the Holy Spirit—the gift of Christ at Pentecost—fell on only devout Jews and God-fearers (Acts 2:1-13). But then an unprecedented event occurred: the Holy Spirit came upon Gentiles who had come to believe in the way of Jesus, *before they were initiated into the covenant through circumcision*:

> The Holy Spirit fell on everyone who heard the word. The circumcised believers who had come with Peter were astonished that the gift of the Holy Spirit had been poured out even on the Gentiles. They heard them speaking in other languages and praising God. Peter asked, "These people have received the Holy Spirit just as we have. Surely no one can stop them from being baptized with water, can they?" He directed that they be baptized in the name of Jesus Christ. (Acts 10:44-48a)

But just as had been true regarding food laws, it was not only *the event itself* that changed the church. It was *the discernment of the community*—the *holy conversation*—that followed.

The first step was for firsthand witnesses, including the Apostle Peter, to take their *testimony* to other believers in Jerusalem. They shared their experience, which no doubt took courage, since they knew how controversial their witness would be.

The second step was for the *conversation* to take place. Initially, those who hear it are appalled (Acts 11:3). But notice how Peter reacts: rather than attack his accusers, or just walk away from the community, he takes them seriously and continues to testify. Step-by-step, Peter lays out the chain of events that led to his decision to baptize the Gentiles (11:4-17). He recognizes that it's against the Hebrew scripture. He turns to the words of Jesus for authority: "When I began to speak, the Holy Spirit fell on them, just as the Spirit fell on us in the beginning. I remembered the Lord's words: 'John will baptize with water, but you will be baptized with the Holy Spirit'" (11:15-16). Finally, he yields to the experience of the community, ending with the question: "If God gave them the same gift he gave us who believed in the Lord Jesus Christ, then who am I? Could I stand in God's way?" (11:17).

The third step was for those gathered in Jerusalem to *listen* and take to heart what Peter said. They were still baffled, but they took him at his word: "Once the apostles and other believers heard this, they calmed down" (Acts 11:18).

Finally, they came to *a shared conclusion*: "They praised God and concluded, 'So then God has enabled Gentiles to change their hearts and lives so that they might have new life'" (Acts 11:18).

Was this the end of the story? Hardly! It shouldn't surprise us that a matter of this gravity would not be quickly settled. Just four chapters later, in Acts 15, deep disagreement over circumcision is still weighing heavily on the community: "Some people came down from Judea teaching the family of believers, 'Unless you are circumcised according to the custom we've received from Moses, you can't be saved'" (Acts 15:1). This time it's not Peter but Paul and Barnabas who make their case against requiring circumcision.

They had been on a joint mission to the Gentiles when they returned to Jerusalem:

> The church at Antioch appointed Paul, Barnabas, and several others from Antioch to go up to Jerusalem to set this question before the apostles and the elders. . . . They gave a full report of what God had accomplished through their activity. Some believers from among the Pharisees stood up and claimed, "The Gentiles must be circumcised. They must be required to keep the Law from Moses." (Acts 15:2b-5)

Why did the Judean Christians demand circumcision? Because they cherished the Law they had inherited and experienced the liberation that fidelity to God's covenant offered. They found it freeing to separate themselves from the polluting influences of the sensual, indulgent culture. They were clear about their priorities, and they believed in conservative values, not for the sake of nostalgia or legalism but because they were faithful to the authority of scripture. They trusted that the way of God was life-giving.

How did these two groups of Jesus's followers—on the one hand those proselytizing the Gentiles and on the other the stricter Judean believers—resolve their differences? Scripture tells us that they had another go at *coming together to discern* (Acts 15:6-11).

How did they do it? First, each one *testified*. Each leader took a turn speaking to the issue: first Peter, then Paul and Barnabas, then James. Next, *they conversed together*. They took to heart each other's testimony and the reality of their own experience, the evidence of the Holy Spirit, the authority of scripture, and the teachings of Jesus. Third, *they listened* to each other: "The entire assembly fell quiet as they listened to Barnabas and Paul describe all the signs and wonders God did among the Gentiles through their activity" (Acts 15:12). They turned to the *authority of Scripture, Christ, and the Spirit*, and, in the end, they *came to a conclusion*: they determined that there were indeed portions of the Law of Moses that would be required: "avoid the pollution associated with food offered to idols, sexual immorality, eating meat from strangled animals, and consuming blood" (15:20). Yet, later, as we've seen with food offered to idols, even some of these requirements also fell, as the process of discernment continued on.

It's also instructive to notice what the early Christians did *not* do. Even though they were deeply divided, they tried not to throw stones at each other. They did not go public with press releases. They did not discard each other's witness as irrelevant. They didn't disown each other. They tried not to attack each other. Instead, they testified and listened. In a later chapter we'll explore just how crucial this is in our witness to the world. But for now let's focus on how it impacted the Christian community.

It wasn't easy going forward. Paul's letter to the Galatians indicates that intense disagreements remained. He reminded dissenters of the decisions made at the Jerusalem Council:

> James, Cephas [Simon Peter], and John, who are considered to be key lead-ers, shook hands with me and Barnabas as equals when they recognized the grace that was given to me. So it was agreed that we would go to the Gentiles, while they continue to go to the people who were circumcised. They asked only that we would remember the poor, which was certainly something I was willing to do. (Gal 2:9-10)

For those who wanted to continue the rite of circumcision among the Jewish followers of Jesus, it was fine; but they should not require it of pagans. At times, Paul grew accusatory about motive: "Whoever wants to look good by human standards will try to get you to be circumcised, but only so they won't be harassed for the cross of Christ" (Gal 6:12). At times, he grew fiercely defensive: "I wish that the ones who are upsetting you would castrate them-selves!" (Gal 5:12).

Why was he so upset? Because he felt that the *adiaphora* (indifferent things) of circumcision was getting in the way of the *esse* (essential things) of Christ's commands: "Being circumcised or not being circumcised doesn't matter in Christ Jesus, but faith working through love does matter" (Gal 5:6).

Did that mean "anything goes"? Hardly. Paul, who himself had once subscribed to Pharisaic purity and rigor, deeply appreciated God's gift of scripture's laws (Phil 3:5). He combated licentiousness: "Should we continue sinning so grace will multiply? Absolutely not!" (Rom 6:1-2a; see also 1 Cor 5). But in the end, he summed up the Christian life this way: "We know that a person isn't made righteous by the works of the Law but rather through the faithfulness of Jesus Christ" (Gal 2:16a). Rather than looking to circumcision as the sign and evidence of covenant life, Paul looked for the gifts of the Holy Spirit: "The fruit of the Spirit is love, joy, peace, patience, kindness, goodness, faithfulness, gentleness, and self-control" (Gal 5:22-23).

Ironically, it ended up that some of these same questions started being addressed within the Jewish community too. In the interconnected Empire, things were changing, and Jewish leaders began to disagree about what to do about converts. Rabbis Joshua ben Hannania and Eliezer ben Hyrcanus were influential around the same time the Gospels were written, following the destruction of the Temple in 70 CE. Their opinions, recorded in the Babylonian Talmud, give us a glimpse into the arguments among Jewish leaders: Rabbi Joshua says that if a proselyte is immersed but not circumcised this is valid, because our mothers were immersed but not circumcised. Rabbi Eliezer says the opposite, because such was found regarding our fathers.[6] In our time, we're embroiled in different—but no less painful—arguments. It's encouraging that even among the earliest Christians, their difficult discernment wasn't instantly wrapped up neatly with a bow. Instead, as Jesus's followers sorted through their beloved Jewish inheritance, they had painfully hard work to do. They considered the story they received, the values it reflected, the memories it carried. They discerned what the next generation needed most to receive: of Jewish identity and struggles, triumphs, and hard-won wisdom. For everything, they had choices to make: Which elements of worship and practice, beliefs and values were obviously so important that they needed to keep them? And what, in the end, didn't matter? Some of the answers they came up with were obvious; others were startling.

And the same will be true for us. Cryptomnesia tricks us into thinking this is new territory. But the work ahead of us is remarkably similar to the work the early church once did: to sort through what we've received and discern what is central (*esse*) and what is indifferent (*adiaphora*).

Worship, Behavior, and Belief: Sorting What's Essential Today

Much as my family had to discern what was precious about my mother's possessions, the church today has important work to do sorting through our inheritance of faith. It can be tempting to try to hang on to everything. But we can't hang on to every last piece. Doing so would weigh us down and prevent us from moving forward. Organization expert Peter Walsh knows this; on his show *Extreme Clutter*, he helps people burdened by too much stuff sort through and let go of their things. In one episode he summed up his philosophy this way: "When *everything's* important, I say, *nothing* is important."[7]

We can't keep everything. If we tried, we'd be building a museum—not cherishing our legacy. My colleague in the presbytery of Chicago, associate executive presbyter Jan Edmiston, puts it this way:

> We in the institutional church have loved many things more than we've loved God. We love our camps, our stained glass windows, our pipe organs, our Sunday School traditions, our buildings, our women's groups, our pastors, and our hymnals more than we've loved God. This makes Jesus slap his hand to his head.
>
> We in the institutional church need to remember why we exist. Do we exist to please ourselves? (*"But I love the old hymns." "But I love Vacation Bible School." "But I love it when men wear ties to church."*) Or do we exist to make disciples of all nations and to love God and neighbor?[8]

How do we begin to recognize what's *really* important and what we can leave behind?

Let's start with worship. Like the earliest Christians who inherited patterns of faith—including scripture and prayer, rituals and music—how do we discern what to keep and what to let go of?

"Worship wars" is the term that has captured the distressing tension churches have experienced these last few decades.[9] One leader describes them as "The Good Old Hymns vs. Modern Worship Choruses; Organ & Piano vs. Those Demon Drums."[10] I would add: steady pews versus auditorium seating, formal robes versus casual jeans, paper bulletins versus flashy screens.

This sorting hasn't been easy! Not because we all love everything we inherited from "the good old days" in worship. It's been hard because, like my mother's possessions, so many things have memories associated with them. Depending on our generation and how long we've been "churched," we might remember singing "A Mighty Fortress" or "In the Garden," "Kumbaya" or "Let There Be Peace on Earth." I still recall putting on my Easter bonnet, sipping from a tiny glass cup at my first Communion, hearing the sonorous deep voice of the preacher thundering from the pulpit in his black robe. My friend Rick Spalding grew up in the church where I now serve. He hadn't been here for decades, but a few years ago he came to visit. As soon as he walked into the sanctuary he gasped: the beautiful Tiffany window that graces the front of the church, Rick said, "is where I first learned that Jesus loved me." These memories are formative, and they stir in us still.

Yet, as we've seen the vernacular of American culture change, not everything that was meaningful to my parents' generation has continued to speak to their grandchildren's generation. My church boasts a massive Casavant Frères pipe organ, which our organist masterfully plays on Sunday morning; and in every pew rack rest copies of *Glory to God*, the newest hymnal published by the Presbyterian Church (USA). Yet, every Sunday evening at our "first@five" service, a screen goes up for YouTube clips and the words to hymns, a bank of candles is set up for our Taizé-style opening, the piano and mikes get rolled into the corner for folk-rock musicians to step in, and the

Communion table comes down the steps from the chancel into the nave so it's among the people. Especially with a college across the street from us, worship at First Church needs to be multilingual.

People in the American church are not the only ones adapting to disorienting cultural change. The shrinking world cuts both ways. When one of my parishioner's parents helped establish a school for handicapped children in Tanzania, our church gladly stepped in to support it. On our first visit to the mission, my friend showed us around a nearby vocational school. We were impressed with the classrooms that trained young people as electricians, tailors, and woodworkers. Then the school director showed us another classroom where children learned to build pipe organs. They apparently are all the rage in local churches, introduced by German Lutheran mission workers. Pipe organs! I would never have guessed.

Yet, in the midst of all this change, there *are* essential things in worship that we've kept from one generation to the next. In fact, *they are exactly the same things that our earliest Christian brothers and sisters once deemed crucial two millennia ago*: scripture and interpretation, prayers, and the sacraments of Communion and baptism. These are *esse*—so central to our faith that we cannot worship without them.

Other aspects of worship may be precious to us personally. Perhaps they conveyed the gospel to our hearts, as the Tiffany window did for my friend Rick. Perhaps they connect us to the saints of other generations, the way "A Mighty Fortress" links us to the Reformation or "In the Garden" reminds me of my grandmother, who loved that song. But in the end, these particular places and music are *adiaphora*: they are wonderful, but *they are not essential to carrying the gospel to the next generation*. Earlier this year I attended the funeral of another pastor. This pastor was a wonderful man, and his service was simply magnificent. We heard the word proclaimed and brilliantly interpreted. We fervently joined in prayer and participated in the renewal of our own baptismal vows as we celebrated his baptism made complete. Then, at the end of worship, the superb organist played Widor's *Toccata*. We all sat to appreciate the testimony of his music, a witness of hope and strength and endurance. Yet I could not help but wonder: if I am ever blessed with grandchildren, will they hear the Widor *Toccata*? I can't know, and though I'd like very much if they did, what matters most is that they know the love of God for them in Jesus Christ.

In the United States, worship wars have been going on for over thirty years. As painful as they've been, we've ended up in a remarkably clear place. Our divisions over music, room design, leaders' garb, and worship guides are decidedly *adiaphora*. We will all have our preferences and may even still squabble over them. But I don't know anyone who believes anymore that those features of worship are *esse*—essential to the faith.

If it was tender and sorrowful for us to go through worship wars, we are now experiencing an even more brutal division over ethics and behavior. Disagreements over sexual expression and conduct are dividing congregations and splintering denominations. As we try to sort this out, we need to clear the cobwebs that cryptomnesia has placed in our memories.

Remembering the steps the church took in its earliest years can help us move forward today:

- They came *together* to discern.

- They took turns *testifying*.

- They *listened* to each other's witness.

- They looked to the *authority* of scripture, Jesus's teachings, and the Holy Spirit.

In the next chapter we'll delve deeper into issues of authority. But for now, let's turn to the crucial work of coming together to witness and to listen.

One of the first things I've learned over years of providing family and premarital counseling is that it takes commitment to come together. It takes courage to speak up. But above all, it takes dedication to listen to each other. As the great twentieth-century theologian Paul Tillich is reported to have said, "The first duty of love is to listen."

Why is listening so hard? Sometimes we assume we already know what the other person is going to say. Sometimes we're so eager to make our own point that we can't wait for the other to finish. Sometimes we're so convinced that the other doesn't understand us that we keep hammering our words home. Sometimes we're so hurt that we can't let down our guard to really listen or share. Sometimes we don't trust that the other cares. Sometimes we miss the underlying values behind the other's point of view.

How do you get beyond these obstacles? Louisville Seminary president Michael Jinkins suggests the practice of "intellectual empathy":

> Practicing intellectual empathy is a kind of spiritual discipline, because it necessitates that we put aside our belief that the lens through which we view the world is the only right one (see Rom 12:3). In intellectual empathy we do not sacrifice critical thinking, but before we move to offer critique, we first hear others thoughtfully and try to imagine what it would be like to share their convictions.[11]

Intellectual empathy isn't easy, Jinkins reminds us: "Genuine intellectual empathy requires creativity and commitment—a commitment and a willingness to imagine others' ideas from within, even if you disagree."[12]

I would encourage us to practice emotional empathy as well—to try to enter into each other's hearts. In counseling, I invite couples to repeat back the words the person has said—*and discern the feelings beneath them.* An initial conversation might go like this:

> Wife: "I am so tired of you never being around for the kids. We had these kids together, but I'm in this alone!"

> Husband, first try: "But I'm trying to make money to support our family!"

With practice over time, understanding grows:

Husband, second try: "You wish I were around more."

Husband, third try: "You feel like you're left by yourself as a single parent to care for our children. I guess you long for me to be your partner again!"

Coming together to speak with courage and listen with empathy is the first work for a family divided, and the same is true for the family of faith. A few years ago, at a meeting among Presbyterian pastors divided on the issue of gay ordination, things shifted palpably when one of the representatives on the liberal end of things said to her conservative brothers, "Let's see if I understand. You feel like our press for gay ordination—our insistence in coming back with overtures year after year—is telling you that scripture doesn't matter, our fellowship doesn't matter, and you don't matter, and we'd gladly burn the whole thing down as long as we get our way until you go away." "Yes, that's right." "And furthermore, you feel that your belief that gay ordination is wrong doesn't come out of homophobia but comes from your love for scripture and a desire to obey our Lord Jesus." "Exactly."

The same is true in the reverse. When a conservative Christian is able to say to his progressive counterpart, "I know that you love the Lord," or, "I can see that you love scripture, but we disagree on these passages," or, "You cherish the church's teachings, but you feel that homosexuals are wired this way and made in the image of God too, and it would be *unnatural* for them to behave otherwise," then the other's testimony has been heard and the work of discernment can begin.

In the end, I suspect that we will come to the same conclusion about sexual orientation that the early church did about circumcision. It will not be seen as *esse*—essential. This is the conclusion that Ken Wilson has come to. Ken, the founding pastor of the Vineyard Church in Ann Arbor, Michigan, recently published *A Letter to my Congregation: An Evangelical Pastor's Path to*

Embracing People Who Are Gay, Lesbian and Transgender into the Company of Jesus. Reviewer Bill Tammeus writes:

> Wilson is well aware that many, if not most, Christians who would call themselves evangelical or conservative still believe homosexuality is a sin—or at least that homosexual acts are sinful. . . . So he is careful not to dismiss such thinking without leaving some room for finding ways for Christians who disagree about this to live together in reasonable harmony.
>
> For the purpose of living with disagreement (which he calls a third way forward), he relies on chapters 14 through 16 of the Apostle Paul's letter to the Romans in the New Testament. There, Wilson says, Paul describes "disputable matters" within the community of followers of Jesus. That, Wilson says, is a model for us now, meaning we should be able simply to call the question of homosexuality a disputable matter and not insist that everyone agree today on how to handle it. Eventually it will work itself out.
>
> . . . The question of homosexuality may not, in fact, be a "disputable matter" to people who are convinced they are right on the issue, but their willingness to call it that and live peacefully with people who disagree with them would be a sign of love and of a commitment to the unity of the church: "A true unity of the Spirit is possible," Wilson writes, "without adopting a common perspective on this question."[13]

That's my prayer too. And I pray that we get there by continuing to engage in holy conversations starting with *testimony*—having the courage to say what we sincerely believe is of the Spirit, even if it's controversial. Second, *we converse together*. Discernment doesn't happen in a vacuum. Third, *we listen to each other* not just for show but also out of love for Christ, whom we serve. Only then can *we come to a conclusion*, knowing that our conclusion may end up being challenged and changing again over time, just as it did for the early church.

In the end, there will inevitably be things over which we disagree. It has always been that way in Christ's family. From the beginning in the early church, and over the course of Christian history, believers have argued vehemently over myriad issues: what is permissible to eat and drink (from pork to Prohibition); what clothing and hairstyles befit Christians (from veils on women's heads to jeans in church); what music to sing and what language to speak in worship (from Gregorian chants to pipe organs and praise bands; from speaking in tongues to the Latin Mass); how to raise funds for the poor and pay for leaders' expenses (from Paul's appeals to pew rentals and capital campaigns); and much, much more. Among Christians around the world today, the range of beliefs, behaviors, and worship styles is staggering.

The wonder is that we agree on so much of what we received from our "mother church." Yet perhaps it should not surprise us. It is the same, strong heart of Christ that for millennia has pumped lifeblood throughout his body: the tenacious love of God, the wondrous grace of Jesus Christ, the sanctifying work of the Holy Spirit, and the building up of community—all attested to by the enduring word of scripture. These are *esse*—essential things—that shall endure forever.

Chapter 4

Authority and Community in a Flattened Age

Question *authority.* The phrase may have started with the hippies in the 1960s, but it has only gained steam. Now that we're connected by the Internet, informed by the World Wide Web, and given voice in social media, people are free to form their own opinions regardless of social norms. No one can stop them.

For many, this trend is immensely empowering. It galvanizes ordinary people to stand up to oppression and injustice. Soon after Hosni Mubarak was thrown out as Egypt's autocratic president early in 2011, one of my church members traveled to Saudi Arabia for a business meeting. He told me everyone was whispering, "Nasser was poisoned, Sadat assassinated; Mubarak was Facebooked." Reporter Lev Grossman described the role Twitter played in protests in Iran:

> When protests started to escalate, and the Iranian government moved to suppress dissent both on- and off-line, the Twitterverse exploded with tweets from people who weren't having it. . . . While the front pages of Iranian newspapers were full of blank space where censors had whited-out news stories, Twitter was delivering information from street level, in real time.[1]

And when fifteen-year-old Malala Yousafzai was shot at point-blank range by the Taliban for daring to go to school, no one expected her to survive. Instead, she has taken her story from a remote valley in Pakistan to the halls of the United Nations and beyond.[2] Oppressive regimes can no longer silence people.

"Through the power of technology, age-old obstacles to human interaction, like geography, language and limited information, are falling and a new wave of human creativity and potential is rising," note Eric Schmidt and Jared Cohen in *The New Digital Age*. "Mass adoption of the Internet is driving one of the most exciting social, cultural and political transformations in history."[3]

Yet we can also predict that the same decline of authority that frees individuals to stand up to injustice may pose a threat to well-ordered society: "Consider too what the lack of top-down control allows," warn Schmidt and Cohen: "the online scams, the bullying campaigns, the hate-group websites and the terrorist chat rooms."[4]

We've seen the downside of authority's decline in American life today—not just in external threats from terrorists but internally too. Teachers and sports referees are taken to task by parents who are unhappy about their children's grades or a call in the game. Police officers are called "pigs" and worse. Then there's the scathing arena of politics. "We are in an era of incivility," is how one political scientist sums up the erosion of respect for our elected officials. Many of us remember when South Carolina representative Joe Wilson yelled, "You lie," during President Obama's State of the Union address. (He later offered the president an apology.)[5] Whether or not one agrees with the president, respect for the authority of the office used to be assumed. It's not anymore.

What happened? Authority that was once taken for granted is being dismantled. For good or ill, the breakdown of authority is a predictable—perhaps inevitable—outcome of our vastly interconnected age. "The Internet is the largest experiment involving anarchy in history," say Schmidt and Cohen.[6]

Access to information, resources, and people infinitely increases individuals' choices and flattens power.

Indeed, "the world is flat" is how journalist Thomas L. Friedman put it in his book by that title. How we respond to this flattening of authority will vary widely depending on our circumstance and worldview:

> Some people will respond with a sense of exhilaration and freedom—seeing an opportunity to soar, expand, dig, or build in any direction with a whole new set of tools. Others will react with the anxiety of people in free fall, with nothing to hold them up or in place. Some will feel liberated, others totally disoriented.[7]

Disoriented is the perfect word for what many people are feeling. It's like an earthquake, bringing down walls and shaking the foundation that under-pins social norms. Friedman says: "Anthropologists and historians tell us that rapid social change is highly destabilizing. . . . It is becoming stressful already. The old boundaries . . . are going, and we do not yet know exactly what will replace them."[8] It's true for political life, commercial interactions, educational systems, and every other social sphere, which includes, of course, the church.

We've already seen the unprecedented decline in the numbers who turn to religious affiliation for guidance. One-fifth of Americans of all ages and one-third of adults under thirty claim "none" as their religious affiliation. All measures are down, from worship attendance to the degree of importance of religion in their lives.[9] Some have dismissed the authority of the church because of distrust and corruption—the abuse by Roman Catholic priests comes to mind. Others have simply walked away from organized religion because it no longer carries weight for them, or they're sampling from the global smorgasbord of spiritual options.

Perhaps even more remarkably, even those who *do* claim Christianity as their faith question traditional authority. As Diana Butler Bass testifies: "Indeed, when people share their faith stories, they often start with 'I don't think that the pope really speaks for God,' 'I can't recite the creed anymore because I just don't believe it,' or 'I can no longer say that Jesus is the only way to heaven.'"[10]

Where do we turn for authority in times like this? Having *some* kind of authority isn't optional; it's essential for us as social creatures. "We are all still human beings," Friedman reminds us, "and . . . we need agreed-upon norms of behavior and rules of commerce. We need agreed-upon ways of establishing authority and building communities, doing work, protecting copyrights, and determining whom to trust."[11]

When authority has been dismantled, and we try to discern among all of the choices we're offered, what do we do? How do we navigate our way forward? We're fortunate that the church has experience with this already, even if cryptomnesia has clouded our memories. The first Christians lived through a very similar upending of authority. Let's rediscover what they learned as we find our way today.

Finding Authority in Community among the Early Christians

The early Christians who experienced the unsettling impact of Roman roads knew this kind of upheaval. As scholar Julie Galambush reminds us, questioning authority was rampant among the Jewish population at this time. Some of it was for good reason:

Reverence for temple and tradition, like a love of flag and country, [did] not preclude resentment or anger against those in charge of traditional institutions. Corruption in high priestly circles was widely known, and generations of abuses by Roman governors as well as Judean kings had taken a toll on public morale. The tax burden under the Romans was high—as much as 25 percent of a farmer's produce might be owed directly to Rome (plus whatever was collected by client kings). And the system known as tax farming, in which individuals bought the right to collect taxes due to Rome, meant that in every region someone made his living from whatever he could collect *in addition* to the official taxes. Tax farmers were ordinarily drawn from the local citizenry, in this case Jews, thus furthering division and resentment within the community. . . .

Torah, temple and land still commanded respect. Rulers were a different matter.[12]

Just as it is today, authority was suspect when it was seen as corrupt and oppressive. But in addition—just like today—authority was also undermined by the overwhelming number of options people had. As we've already seen, within Judaism, those competing for authority included scribes and Pharisees, Sadducees and Essenes, priests and Zealots. Each group would have others believe that theirs was the one representing the faithful Jewish perspective.

But Roman roads also put people in touch with options *beyond* Judaism. Their tradition was no longer the only game in town. Indeed, more choices were within reach than they'd ever known before. Suddenly, they could pick for themselves which brand of spirituality worked for them. Numerous philosophical movements were part of the competition too: Neoplatonists and Gnostics, Stoics and Epicureans all promised the "good life" to those who would subscribe to their perspective. One historian captures the feeling of disorientation people were experiencing then:

The sense of isolation, rootlessness and insecurity was however strong enough to set people looking for a rule of life which would give them a sense of inward security and stability. This the new philosophies of the Hellenistic period proceeded to supply. They differ in their recipes, but they all claim to give to their followers the same good under different names, a self-sufficient, imperturbable tranquillity proof against all the shocks and changes of Fortune, the shifting restless insecurity of human affairs.[13]

Should it surprise us that faithful Jews sometimes chose from this buffet of options outside their tradition? The prolific writer Philo of Alexandria (20 BCE–45 CE), for example, ascribed to the Law of Moses, counted circumcision essential, and painstakingly interpreted biblical texts. But he was also formed by an assortment of ideas sampled from various philosophical schools. In Philo's day, which was, of course, the time of Jesus and the birth of the church, the mix of nations and flux of ideas fostered this eclectic smorgasbord, suggests one historian: "Platonism, Stoicism, and Neo-Pythagoreanism contributed complementary elements to the general intellectual atmosphere of the time. . . . Philo, with no great discrimination, selects from his knowledge of pagan thought any argument that will serve his turn."[14]

How on earth did the early church deal with this cacophony of voices claiming authority? Anyone who reads the New Testament may be so familiar with the way the early church emerged that it's hard to imagine it developing along any other path. But as we've just seen, there were myriad sources of knowledge, patterns of ethics, and expressions of spirituality in the Greco-Roman world. How did they decide what warranted attention, and what was outside the bounds of faith?

Unlike some of their contemporaries, they were deeply committed to being in community. They were not just *individual* disciples of Jesus Christ. They were part of his body, the church. So each of them deciding whatever they pleased wasn't going to work. This was no small thing. The Greco-Roman culture enthusiastically embraced individualism, freedom of opinion, and the liberty to travel, do commerce, think, act, and worship as any person pleased. With the vast array of options available, why would anyone choose to suppress one's freedom? In part because they discovered the downside of independence: the isolation and loneliness of trying to figure everything out by oneself. One of the greatest gifts the early church inherited from Judaism was the strong, deeply imbedded value of community: the knowledge that we need each other.

But not all communities are the same. How would they be structured, and who would have authority to lead them? There were so many different models of authority in communities in the Greco-Roman world: What course would they choose?

The Synagogue

The synagogue was the first model to follow. As we've already seen, the early Christians gathered in private homes for scripture and interpretation, prayers and common meals. These "house churches" were named for the original convert or for the patron whose home was large enough for the gathering and whose resources might fund expenses. The households of Lydia (Acts 16:15), Crispus (Acts 18:8), Stephanas (1 Cor 1:16; 16:15), Onesiphorus (2 Tim 1:16), Prisca and Aquila (1 Cor 16:19), and even some members of the emperor's household (Phil 4:22) are cited by name. Just as we have "First Methodist Church" or "Trinity Lutheran Church," they would consider themselves members of "Lydia's household" or "Onesiphorus's household." And all of them belonged to the larger family of Jesus Christ: the "household of God, which is the church of the living God" (1 Tim 3:15 NRSV).

It's notable that as Paul and others reached out to the Gentile community, they didn't adopt synagogue-like titles such as *archisynagogos* ("head-of-synagogue") or *archontes* ("ruler"). Unlike the synagogues, even wealthy patrons, such as Lydia, Prisca, and Aquila, who provided for the Christian community didn't receive special honorifics.[15] But the synagogue was hardly the only model.

Voluntary Associations

Because so many converts to Christianity were Gentile, the early church also had at its disposal the structural patterns of any number of Greco-Roman voluntary associations of the day. One writer describes a "luxuriant growth of clubs, guilds and associations of all sorts"[16] at the time. Some of these groups gathered for civic purposes, much as Rotary or Kiwanis Clubs function for us today. Others were burial associations that gathered to ensure the proper ongoing honor to the deceased. Still others were underground, politically seditious groups. There were even secret societies dedicated to bacchanalia, akin to 1920s speakeasies or 1960s swingers' groups. (By the second century, Christianity's opponents often painted the church as one of these underground clubs.)[17]

The members of the early church would have been familiar with all of these pagan associations and recognized that they didn't reflect the values Jesus taught them. Among other things, most of these groups borrowed titles from municipal offices—treasurer, secretary, and so on—but again, Paul urged the churches not to stratify among higher and lower ranks (see, e.g., 1 Cor 12).[18]

Philosophical Schools: The Ekklesia

But there was yet another model: the Greek philosophical school. By Jesus's day, groups had long formed around various philosophers. Historian Wayne Meeks finds striking parallels between the Jesus movement and the communities who followed Epicurus (341–270 BCE):

> There is much in the life of these [Epicurean] communities that reminds us of the Pauline congregations. Based on "that highly adaptable institution, the Hellenic household," they strove to produce the intimacy of a family among the members, who included male and female, slave and free, bound together by love (*philia*), "the immortal good." There was no rigid hierarchy of office, but some functional differentiation, based on one's stage of advancement in the school's thought.[19]

It is perhaps this kind of household group, or *ekklesia*, that formed the closest parallel to the Christian community.

The Christian Ekklesia

What did the early Christian *ekklesia* look like? It included three crucial rules: valuing each person's gifts, building up the household in love, and aspiring to Christlikeness. Let's look at each of these rules.

First, the church *embraced every individual's gifts*, regardless of civic rank, wealth, gender, or other cultural hierarchy. Rich and poor, educated and unschooled, men and women met together under one roof as equals: witness Paul's testimony that in Christ "there is neither Jew nor Greek; there is neither slave nor free; nor is there male and female" (Gal 3:28). Each person in a household—even servants—was valued for his or her commitment to the way of Jesus.

Why was this flattening of hierarchy so important? Early Christians understood this as central in Jesus's teaching:

> An argument arose among the disciples about which one of them was the greatest. Aware of their deepest thoughts, Jesus took a little child and had the child stand beside him. Jesus said to his disciples, "Whoever welcomes this child in my name welcomes me. Whoever welcomes me, welcomes the one who sent me. Whoever is least among you all is the greatest." (Luke 9:46-48)

In addition, they saw this teaching at work when the Holy Spirit came to everyone. Paul wrote:

> A word of wisdom is given by the Spirit to one person, a word of knowledge to another according to the same Spirit, faith to still another by the same Spirit, gifts of healing to another in the one Spirit, performance of miracles to another, prophecy to another, the ability to tell spirits apart to another, different kinds of tongues to another, and the interpretation of the tongues to another. All these things are produced by the one and same Spirit who gives

what he wants to each person. . . . We were all baptized by one Spirit into one body, whether Jew or Greek, or slave or free, and we all were given one Spirit to drink. (1 Cor 12:8-11, 13)

Rather than one leader being given esoteric rule, as was the case in so many Greco-Roman cults, every Christian carried his or her unique value and authority, a gift from the Holy Spirit. This movement to embrace every person's gifts was a radical move in a highly competitive society. But at a time when many were questioning authority in the world-at-large, many also found the flattening of authority to be attractive.

Yet equality among members also created a new tension. As we all know, no household is exempt from disagreements. Because of the parity of power within the church's structure, it wasn't as if a priest could make a ruling and everybody had to follow it. Since every Christian had authority through the gift of the Holy Spirit, how did they navigate their way through conflict?

This tension was alleviated by the second household rule: this would be *a household built up in love*. This ideal of household love was far more than functional. It was genuinely affectionate. "Especially striking is the language that speaks of the members of the Pauline groups as if they were a family," Wayne Meeks reminds us, and continues:

> They are children of God and also of the apostle. They are brothers and sisters; they refer to one another as "beloved." The Pauline letters are unusually rich in emotional language—joy and rejoicing, anxiety, longing. . . . Both the number and intensity of the affective phrases in the Pauline letters are extremely unusual.[20]

Indeed, Paul constantly addresses fellow Christians not just as "brothers and sisters" but also as "beloved" (e.g., 1 Cor 15:58; 2 Cor 7:1; Eph 5:1; Phil 2:12, and so on). Certain communities, like those in Philippi and Thessalonica, reflected extraordinary intimacy: "We were gentle with you like a nursing mother caring for her own children. We were glad to share not only

God's good news with you but also our very lives because we cared for you so much. . . . You know how we treated each of you like a father treats his own children" (1 Thess 2:7-8, 11).

All this affection wasn't arbitrary or manipulative. It was a reflection of their core understanding of the way of Jesus. All four gospels show Jesus inviting people into the family of God: "Whoever does God's will" and all "who listen to God's word and do it" are "my mother and my brothers" (Mark 3:34-35 and Luke 8:21). And their love for each other was to be as much a sign of the way of Jesus as loving God and neighbor (e.g., Luke 10:27): "I give you a new commandment: Love each other. Just as I have loved you, so you also must love each other. This is how everyone will know that you are my disciples, when you love each other" (John 13:34-35). As we'll explore later, this will prove to be key in their witness to the world.

The believers' striving to love each other reframed the value of each person's gifts: they were intended not to compete for individual glory but to contribute toward the well-being of the household. Indeed, the activator of the Spirit's gifts for their *proper* usage is love. Otherwise, they're empty and moot. Even though the culture prized particular skills—especially preaching (like a well-spoken philosopher), as well as speaking in tongues and prophesying (popular in mystery religions)—Paul was clear that, for followers of Jesus, personal success was beside the point. As Paul wrote in the famous passage so often used at weddings:

> If I speak in the tongues of human beings and of angels but I don't have love, I'm a clanging gong or clashing cymbal. If I have the gift of prophecy and I know all the mysteries and everything else, and if I have such complete faith that I can move mountains but I don't have love, I'm nothing. If I give away everything that I have and hand over my own body to feel good about what I've done but I don't have love, I receive no benefit whatsoever. (1 Cor 13:1-3)

The authority of spiritual gifts was found not in their razzle-dazzle but in their contribution to the "common good" of the household of God (1 Cor

12:7). Not everyone opted into this commitment. "Demas has fallen in love with the present world and has deserted me," Paul wrote (2 Tim 4:10). Demas would have hardly been the only one to do so, given the endless array of spiritual options the culture was all too glad to provide.

This leads to the third rule of the household: *aspiring to Christlikeness* rather than personal glory or the values of the present world. To the Romans, Paul wrote:

> Don't be conformed to the patterns of this world, but be transformed by the renewing of your minds so that you can figure out what God's will is—what is good and pleasing and mature. Because of the grace that God gave me, I can say to each one of you: don't think of yourself more highly than you ought to think. Instead, be reasonable since God has measured out a portion of faith to each one of you. (Rom 12:2-4)

Maturity in Christ was the ultimate point for the household of God. Even though different roles quickly developed in the *ekklesia*, their purpose was not competitive or hierarchical but to help everyone in the household grow more and more in the pattern and image of Christ:

> He gave some apostles, some prophets, some evangelists, and some pastors and teachers. His purpose was to equip God's people for the work of serving and building up the body of Christ until we all reach the unity of faith and knowledge of God's Son. God's goal is for us to become mature adults—to be fully grown, measured by the standard of the fullness of Christ. (Eph 4:11-13; see also 1 Cor 12:8-10, 28-30; Rom 12:6-8)

Was the household of God perfect? Far from it. There was bad behavior: greed, lewdness, idolatry, jealousy (Rom 13:13; 1 Cor 3:3; 1 Tim 3:3). There was gossip and slander (2 Cor 12:20), and Paul himself occasionally became enraged (Gal 5:12). There were constant quarrels and factions (Rom 13:13; 14:1; 1 Cor 1:11; 3:3; 2 Cor 12:20; Gal 5:20; 1 Tim 3:3; 2 Tim 2:23-24; Titus 3:2, 9). These were more than mere distractions. They were evidence of immaturity in Christ. For all the while, the goal remained the same: to grow into the likeness of Christ, manifesting his spiritual gifts, above all, "love . . . shown without pretending" (Rom 12:9).

Authority in Christian Community Today

The lack of authority in the spiritual life of Americans today is not unlike the free-for-all the world experienced at the time of the earliest Christians. The standards, beliefs, and disciplines that mainline denominations long provided are no longer honored by the culture. And even many within the church freely question authority.

Remember sociologist Robert Bellah, who introduced us to "Sheilaism" to describe the individualistic American religious consumer? ("Sheila," whom we met in chapter 1, was the one who defined her faith as "my own Sheilaism": "It's just try to love yourself and be gentle with yourself. You know, I guess, take care of each other."[21]) Well, Bellah wants us to know that do-it-yourself faith is no longer just for the unchurched: Based on interviews and other data, he suspects that many worshipers in American churches are "Sheilaists" who approach faith as a matter of personal opinion. They feel little or no influence from scripture, tradition, or the historic church. In fact,

> 80 percent of Americans agreed with the statement that "an individual should arrive at his or her own religious beliefs independent of any churches or synagogues." Now, again, that isn't the way it really happens. But just the notion that religious belief ought to be a purely internal thing, and then you go to the church or synagogue of your choice, shows how deeply ingrained a kind of religious privatism is, which turns the church into something like the Kiwanis Club or some other kind of voluntary association that you go to or not if you feel comfortable with it—but which has no organic claim upon you.[22]

If Bellah is right, then "Sheilaism" suggests that there could be a different religion for every single American. If that was true thirty years ago, how much more is it the case today, when everyone has virtual access to every world religion through his or her iPad or cell phone! Indeed, Eric Schmidt and Jared Cohen remind us, "By 2025, the majority of the world's population will, in one generation, have gone from having virtually no access to unfiltered information to accessing all of the world's information through a device that fits in the palm of the hand."[23]

Yet having *some* kind of authority and mutual accountability is still essential for life together. To reiterate Thomas Friedman's point, human beings "need agreed-upon norms of behavior and rules of commerce. We need agreed-upon ways of establishing authority and building communities, doing work, protecting copyrights, and determining whom to trust."[24]

Voluntary Membership Organizations

So where do we find authority and structure community when tradition, hierarchy, and discipline have been flattened? Like the first-century Christians, today's Christians are surrounded by a variety of models. An obvious parallel is the voluntary membership organization, of which there are many examples: film and book groups, Kiwanis and Rotary Clubs, country clubs, Scouting organizations, sororities and fraternities, Veterans of Foreign Wars, garden clubs, and more. Some, like film clubs, are open to all; some are invitation only, such as fraternities and country clubs. Some are gender-specific, like Scouting and fraternities. Some are based on shared experience or interest, like civic leadership, gardening, military experience, or education.

In every case, there are clear expectations for participation. A film club, for example, might require only sharing one's e-mail address. A country club would require extensive dues, impose a dress code, and restrict cell phone use. Scouting requires pledging allegiance to the American flag and an oath of honor and expects members to participate in weekly meetings and strive for merit badges.

Yet, oddly, it's not membership organizations on which most American churches are patterned. Instead, for many congregations, it is an unlikely suspect: the church as corporation.

Corporations

Religious author Diana Butler Bass describes the rise of church-as-corporation, as American congregations became structured in the manner of twentieth-century corporate enterprises:

> Beginning around 1890, denominations built massive bureaucratic structures, modeling themselves after American businesses, complete with corporate headquarters, program divisions, professional development and marketing departments, franchises (parish churches), training centers, and career tracks. Other than the fact that denominations offered religion as the product, they differed little from other corporations that dominated America in the last century. As a Presbyterian elder once sighed to me, "Our church is like GM, only we sell faith."[25]

That was not an altogether bad model for its time. As Butler Bass notes, this model effectively served to "educate, spiritually enliven, and socially elevate" countless people.[26] But it doesn't anymore. Over time, she says,

> as with other corporations of the same vintage, church executives became too distanced from the regular folks; . . . creativity was strangled by red tape; expenses began to outrun income; and huge facilities needed to be maintained. Faith increasingly became a commodity and membership rolls and money the measures of success. The business of the church replaced the mission of the church. Slowly, then more quickly, customers became disgruntled. Resources declined. Brand loyalty eroded.[27]

And, I would add, the market changed. For much of the twentieth century, people were looking for the product the church had to offer. But over these last few decades, our needs changed dramatically.

Training School

A second model for some American churches is that of a training school—not the close-knit, formative kind that the early Christians patterned themselves after but an Enlightenment-style quest for information. John Dorhauer, conference minister in the United Church of Christ, paints well the picture of seminary-trained clergy and their students-in-the-pew:

> The enlightenment model church educated experts at great expense; examined them at great length to determine their adherence to, acceptance of, and propagation of orthodox teaching and practice; and then rewarded the qualified with authorization and a lifetime of income for giving answers to the religiously unsophisticated and uneducated masses.

But, Dorhauer says, the need has changed now. Postmodern people have unfettered access to information, and they are skeptical of anything that bills itself as universal truth or absolute ethics:

> Your truth is your truth—but I live my life differently. Experts don't help the postmodern resolve internal conflict. . . . The role of clergy as professional arbiter of all things good and wise is not an investment the postmodern church is interested in.[28]

Frank Yamada, president of McCormick Theological Seminary, recognizes this problem too. He calls the Enlightenment-shaped clergy "knowledge priests." Now, he says, it's time to discover what "the priesthood of all believers" might look like in our age when information is available to all.[29]

Ekklesia: The Household of God

If corporate products and Enlightenment education aren't needed now, what is? A. H. Armstrong's earlier description of the first century could just as easily apply to our twenty-first century: "The sense of isolation, rootlessness and . . . the shifting restless insecurity."[30] In times of disorientation and rootlessness, people's deepest need is not another institutional program or class. Just like the early church, our deepest need is to belong and grow in a trustworthy and authentic community, a family, a "household of God." Our deepest need is to have a place where it is safe to be real, where we are known and loved both for our gifts and in spite of our flaws. Our deepest need is to learn to love in Christ's family—to love the Lord our God with all our hearts and minds and strength, and learn to love our neighbors as ourselves. Our deepest need is to belong to a household where we are urged to be our better selves as we seek to grow into the likeness of Jesus Christ.

I'm convinced that, long ago, we were given everything to meet these needs. The early church discovered this in three simple but crucial rules for the household of God: valuing each person's gifts, building up the household in love, and aspiring to Christlikeness.

Let's start with what it might look like to *value each one's gifts*. Whether we're in a tiny community where we think we know everything about each other or a huge congregation of strangers, we can be confident that the Spirit has showered the community with a multiplicity of blessings. It is not just preachers who have gifts for ministry, though there is still a role for them as there always has been. The earliest Christians recognized the need to free up particular people to share the word of God (cf. Acts 6:2; 1 Cor 9:14). But there are many, many other gifts that are needed, too.

I don't know about your church, but one of our tendencies in my church is to fill slots that need to be filled: chair of the personnel committee or director of Vacation Bible School, chair of the annual fund-raising auction or member of the board of trustees. In itself, that's not a bad thing; there's important work to be done. The problem is our *starting place*. We start with the business model of jobs to be filled. Instead, we could start with *the gifts that the Spirit has given.*

We did just that at a staff retreat. Even though we know each other's jobs—and thought we knew each other's gifts—we decided to use the Clifton

StrengthsFinder survey. Developed by Tom Rath, its purpose is to identify and develop people's core skills, talents, and knowledge. The survey comes out of Gallup research, which indicates that "people succeed when they focus on what they do best."[31] I was astonished at what we discovered. We learned, for example, that one colleague has as one of her core strengths "positivity": she can't help but encourage other people. Now I know that when I'm discouraged, she is my go-to colleague to shore me up. And we learned that another pastor has "self-assurance" as one of his top strengths. I can learn from him how to battle my own self-doubt. We learned that another colleague and I both share "strategy" as a top gift. Now I have a partner on staff to take our great ideas and do the detail work that moves them into flesh and blood.

It made me wonder: If my pastoral team was surprised at each other's gifts, and we've worked together every day for years, how much are we missing about our leadership teams and church members? What gifts might be right under our noses that we're unaware of? Instead of starting with the question "What job description needs to be filled?" what if we started with the question that the early Christians asked: "What gifts is the Spirit evidencing in our midst?"

Just asking that question has shifted my awareness of the gifts within my congregation. In the last few months I've discovered that my church includes:

- a recently retired CEO who has a passion for helping young professionals grow in their faith and strengthen their families;

- a mission volunteer whose teenage daughter's issues led her to consider becoming a Stephen Minister;

- a scientist working on pharmaceutical research who also wants to educate people about getting access to experimental cancer treatment;

- a homemaker who used to be an entrepreneur, who now feels called to create opportunities for special-needs young adults.

None of these ministries were being developed by committees. Yet that isn't stopping the Holy Spirit from using these people in remarkable ways. The question I'm asking myself now is how our church structure can be less corporate and more open to the moving of the Spirit, lest we miss what's happening right in front of our noses. I wonder how much this is true in other places too.

Just like the early church, it's crucial that individuals' gifts are recognized not as prizes to be ranked but as blessings to be shared for the well-being of the community. In contrast to the overweening individualism of our culture, the Christian community prizes one another's gifts for what they contribute to the common good (1 Cor 12:7).

That's why, as we seek to discover the gifts that the Spirit is pouring out, it's not just about discovering individual gifts. We'll also discover more ways *to build up the household in love*. In *The Church and the Crisis of Community*, Theresa Latini reminds us of the need for the church to be a place where we learn and practice community in an age of social disconnection:

> The nature of community has changed drastically in the last ten years. We are a mobile society. We uproot our families more frequently than former generations did. We connect with friends, family members, and coworkers through electronic communication. Adolescents and young adults form faceless relationships.
>
> Congregations try to sustain community in an era of competing truths, distrust of religious authorities and traditions, and widespread conflict about basic Christian beliefs and practices. . . . Such widespread changes in our experience of community lead to pervasive feelings of uncertainty and anxiety, because all of us have a basic need for belonging and trust, for a community in which we discover ourselves and God's intention for our lives.[32]

Sustaining intimate, accountable Christian relationships in faith communities is crucial. How do we get there? I suspect there will be different models for various communities.

For many congregations, a key place for this to happen is in small-group ministries. These groups will take varying forms in different contexts. They will differ in their longevity: in some churches, these are deeply imbedded groups that have shared history for decades; and in others, they're more fluid, inviting new people in and understanding when members drift off toward a different ministry. They will differ in their makeup: some churches encourage organizing by gender, marital status, or age-range, while others emphasize mixed groups. They will differ in their expectations: some groups require a heavy commitment of homework or even covenant vows, while others are more "come as you are," drop-in friendly. Regardless, Theresa Latini suggests, their care helps the whole church grow as God's family:

> When small groups live the way of the cross in mutual care, practice confession and mutual forbearance, and reflect the unity and diversity of *koinonia*, they help the church grow in mutual integration and edification. When small groups nurture generosity, compassion, and openness to the world and find creative ways to witness to God's love in both word and deed, they help the church fulfill its vocation. . . . In the midst of faceless relationships, small groups can point us to the one face that never goes away, the face of God in Jesus Christ. In the context of being uprooted and displaced, small groups become a spiritual family.[33]

What kind of program do small groups engage in? This too varies widely. One sure method for building up the household of God is Bible study. Pastor Shane Stanford reminds us of how crucial it is for postmodern Christians to claim the authority of scripture:

> First, in-depth Bible study provides a means to know and 'love God' . . . Some lessons in Scripture teach us directly about the person, purpose and plan of God, and some teach us about God's work through creation, covenant and community. In the process, in-depth Bible study utilizes Scripture to recalibrate a congregation's view of God and God's people.

Second, in-depth Bible study provides examples of what it means to 'love like God'. From the beginning of Scripture, a narrative of God's tension between righteousness and love unfolds. Deuteronomy 9 reminded us that just across the line from God's justice is God's great love for God's people. By the end of the story, we discover what it means to form a life around our faith in God—particularly through the gift of God's Son, Jesus Christ.

Therefore, I believe (and hope) Scripture draws us not only to God but to one another as well.[34]

While Bible study is the primary focus for small groups, it need not be the only one. Service-oriented groups can also be transformative in building community.

About eight years ago, our church called a pastor for family ministry—a brand-new position in our church. Our new pastor, Patrick Day, immediately noticed that the children's ministry was thriving and the moms' group was going strong but that the dads were pretty much MIA. Being a young dad himself, he understood the pressure fathers were under. Working long hours, showing up for his kids' sports, music, and Scouting events, nurturing his marriage—all these commitments took time. Moreover, joining a church committee or doing homework for Bible study wasn't exactly going to jumpstart these dads' spiritual lives. So Patrick did something completely different. He gathered a group of young dads every Tuesday night *at the local bar* for a very brief Bible study and much longer check-in about how they were doing. How were they living the faith? What were the challenges? Where was Christ in their lives? And then he challenged them to roll up their sleeves in service. They chose the local homeless shelter as their service project. To this day, twice a month these guys get up in the middle of the night to work the breakfast shift at the shelter. They arrive at 3 a.m., pack sack lunches, make a grocery run, cook eggs and sausage, and feed the men at the shelter. And between service days? They still look out for each other—listening to each other struggle with marriage or faith, pressing each other to be there for their kids, praying for each other's spiritual growth. They've become brothers to each other in Christ's family.

Maybe your church has groups like that too. In our congregation, the same thing happens in the weekly prayer shawl ministry, as people gather every week to knit, visit, and pray; in the Stephen Ministry program, as participants meet one-on-one with their care receivers and share insights at monthly check-ins; in choir, as members share joys and concerns at the end of rehearsal; in the church basement where, twice each week, a team of volunteers visits while they sort donations for our enormous rummage sale.

Small groups take any number of forms. Yet, whether you're in a tiny church or a huge church, a community with high turnover or families in place over many generations, a rural congregation or an urban mecca, the need is still the same. We children of God long to be known and loved and kept accountable. In the family of Christ, we need to know that we aren't forgotten. We matter to each other, and we matter to the Lord.

Finally, as we grow in the household of God, we don't just stay the same. In our age of limitless choice, we remember that there is one model to which we aspire: we seek to be like Jesus. How do we know what that looks like? Just like the earliest Christians, week after week, we return to the enduring word of scripture and the teachings of Jesus. Instruction and admonition, consolation and wisdom draw us to grow in the likeness of Christ (cf. Col 3:16; 1 Thess 4:18; 5:11, 14; 1 Cor 14:31; Rom 15:14).[35]

Is it easy? Hardly! The spiritual work of forbearance, patience, self-control, and other countercultural practices get a workout in Christian community. We hurt one another, fail in our efforts, and revert to childish patterns far too often. Yet bit by bit, we "build up the body" as we grow in our ability to "speak the truth in love" (Eph 4:11-15), as we own up to our errors and call others to account. We learn how to humble ourselves in transparency and correction. Together we learn to grow in the image of Jesus.

It's no accident that our growth in Christ happens not in isolation but in community. All the parts of the body are needed if we are to grow into the body of Christ. Peter Marty, a Lutheran pastor in Iowa, describes it this way: In a congregation, "you create a community of common people gathered for a holy purpose and united by that sense of purpose." In this commitment, you become more than you could be on your own, Marty says, and "that is the secret gift that unfolds as you become integrated into something that is larger than yourself. You find yourself saying yes to possibilities that you would never otherwise imagine."[36]

As "members of one another" (Eph 4:25), we discover that we are members of something far greater than a human institution. We are members of Christ's own body, his presence in the world. I love the charge attributed to the sixteenth-century Carmelite sister Saint Teresa of Avila:

Christ has no body but yours,
No hands, no feet on earth but yours,
Yours are the eyes with which he looks
Compassion on this world,
Yours are the feet with which he walks to do good,
Christ has no body now on earth but yours.
Yours are the hands, with which he blesses all the world.[37]

The era of top-down authority is over. But that doesn't mean there is *no* authority. There is shared authority through the abundant gifts of the Spirit given to all. There is mutual accountability in the household of Christ. And there's a high calling that shapes everything we do: to grow more and more into the image of Jesus Christ. That's more than enough for us to move ahead toward "a future filled with hope" (Jer 29:11). That's more than enough for us to reach out to the world in Christ's name. In the next chapter we'll explore how we reach out to the world more compassionately and effectively.

Chapter 5
Taking the Message to the Masses

Founded in 1951, the church I grew up—in Community Presbyterian in Mount Prospect, outside of Chicago—was one of thousands of church plants that came to life after World War II. As throngs of baby-boomer families streamed into the suburbs, churches like ours were ready to embrace them. It was an exciting time to be part of burgeoning American Protestantism.

But now it's a different story. For a while, mainline churches thought that we just needed to modernize with the latest music or coffee bar. But that's no longer going to work, cautions pastor and scholar James Emery White:

> Here's the essence of the mistake. "If you build it, they will come." . . . If you spruce church up a bit, musically and stylistically, the unchurched will suddenly stream in your doors and fill your seats. No, they won't. . . . Not if they are truly unchurched, part of the growing number of religious "nones" that make up our modern milieu.

Of course, it is tempting for us to fall into the trap of believing that cultural tweaks will bring people in—that if we only "encourage casual dress, offer Starbucks coffee, play rock music, and then deliver a message in a style similar to the popular speakers of the day"—that, somehow, we will magically turn around our diminishing attendance. But, White warns, "it won't work. And it hasn't worked for at least a decade."[1]

If it's been hard for us to get our heads around this shift, it's no wonder. For 1,700 years the church enjoyed "If you build it, they will come." Since 312 CE, when Constantine declared the Empire to be Christian, the church and state have been mutually supportive, largely interwoven enterprises. "Christendom" is what scholars call this long era of interdependence between Christianity and culture.

But as we've seen, that era is fading fast, and our post-Christendom era is looking more and more like pre-Christendom once did. Notice the shifts that happened en route to Christendom and now, in the opposite direction:

SHIFT INTO CHRISTENDOM:	SHIFT INTO POST-CHRISTENDOM:
1. Movement of the church and the Christian story from the margins to the center of society.	1. Movement of the church and Christian story from the center to the margins of society.
2. The development of a culture based on Christian values and traditions, including imposition, by legislation and custom, of Christian morality on the entire society.	2. The dominant culture no longer ascribes to Christian values and traditions. Custom and legislation shift to reflect religious and moral diversity.
3. All citizens (except Jews) are assumed to be Christian by birth, and baptism is the obligatory incorporation into Christian society.	3. Christians may or may not be in the majority, there are numerous spiritual options, and religious choice is a private matter.
4. Sunday as an official holiday and obligatory church attendance, with penalties for non-compliance. Commerce and activities forbidden.	4. "Blue laws" and customs precluding Sunday activities are lifted; church participation is a matter of personal choice.
5. The construction of ornate church buildings, the formation of huge congregations, and the amassing of church wealth.	5. Church buildings are increasingly empty, congregations are dwindling, and finances are at risk.[2]

Not everyplace in America is post-Christendom, by any means. A "post-Christendom continuum" is how John Vest describes it. John, who serves as pastor for youth at Fourth Presbyterian Church in Chicago, offers the continuum as a way of assessing how far down the road a given community might be:

Every community in North America falls somewhere along this continuum. In some places—like rural communities and communities in the American South (where I grew up)—Christianity is still part of the dominant culture. But in other places—like urban centers (where I have spent my entire adult life)—Christianity is no longer embedded in culture as it once was.

I've struggled a bit with what to put on each end of the spectrum to make it understandable and most helpful. With respect to my own experience I will sometimes put my hometown of Niceville, FL on one end—yes, you read that right—and my current city of Chicago on the other end. Sometimes I've used the fictional town of Mayberry. . . .

I've recently discovered that the Barna Group has devoted considerable research to this. . . . According to their research Albany, NY is the most post-Christian city in the nation. Here are the metrics they use:[3]

Post-Christian = meet at least 60% of the following 15 factors (9 or more factors)
Highly Post-Christian = meet at least 80% of the following 15 factors (12 or more factors):
1. do not believe in God
2. identify as atheist or agnostic
3. disagree that faith is important in their lives
4. have not prayed to God (in the last year)
5. have never made a commitment to Jesus
6. disagree the Bible is accurate
7. have not donated money to a church (in the last year)
8. have not attended a Christian church (in the last year)
9. agree that Jesus committed sins
10. do not feel a responsibility to "share their faith"
11. have not read the Bible (in the last week)
12. have not volunteered at church (in the last week)
13. have not attended Sunday school (in the last week)
14. have not attended religious small group (in the last week)
15. do not participate in a house church (in the last year)[4]

For generations, we lived in a Christendom world. All the church had to do was construct a building, hire a pastor, and open the doors: "If you build it, they will come." Now we're missionaries in a secular culture. It's a very different enterprise. Some of us—especially in the South—live in places that still lean heavily toward Christendom. Others—especially in urban centers, the Northeast and the Pacific Northwest—live in decidedly post-Christendom settings. The further into post-Christendom we find ourselves, the more disoriented we feel.

But we've been here before. Cryptomnesia may cloud our memories, but the early church has wisdom to teach us about being Christian in a pluralistic, secular culture. Let us look back and retrieve what we learned in the pre-Christendom age as we seek to live the gospel in our post-Christendom world.

Early Church Engagement with the Culture

Like our cities today, it was the "urban village" where ancient civilizations collided with the greatest frequency. Consider the multiplicity of languages in Jerusalem that we rehearse every year at Pentecost:

> Parthians, Medes, and Elamites; as well as residents of Mesopotamia, Judea, and Cappadocia, Pontus and Asia, Phrygia and Pamphylia, Egypt and the regions of Libya bordering Cyrene; and visitors from Rome (both Jews and converts to Judaism), Cretans and Arabs . . ." (Acts 2:9-11)

And, like today, there was a *range of diversity* within cities across the Empire. Just as Dallas is more religiously homogeneous than Seattle or New York, Jerusalem was extraordinarily homogeneous in comparison to Rome and Athens. Recall this scene in Ostia—the harbor city of ancient Rome (cited in chapter 1):

> The city boasted an astonishing array of religious buildings. Side-by-side with temples to the gods of the Greco-Roman pantheon and the imperial cults

stand Christian baptisteries, a Jewish synagogue, and a host of temples to Near Eastern deities, including a dozen dedicated to the Zoroastrian divinity Mithras, the god of contracts revered by merchants.[5]

While some people were overwhelmed by this cacophony of spiritual options, others were mesmerized by it. Acts 17:21 reports the scene at the Areopagus (Mars Hill) in Athens: "Now all the Athenians and the foreigners living there would spend their time in nothing but telling or hearing something new" (NRSV).

Novelty was highly valued. Just like today, what social psychologists call "FOMO," or "fear of missing out," was rampant. Yet notice how Paul, ever the evangelist, handled the situation in this city that was "flooded with idols" (Acts 17:17-34):

- First, he didn't focus on already-converted Christians to get him to agree with them, nor did he interact exclusively with fellow Jews in the synagogue. Instead, he went to the marketplace (the agora), the center of the city, where the people were: "He also addressed whoever happened to be in the marketplace each day" (v. 17).

- Next, he used the language of the culture rather than Jewish religious terms, even if it meant looking a little foolish: "Certain Epicurean and

Stoic philosophers engaged him in discussion too. Some said, 'What an amateur! What's he trying to say?' Others remarked, 'He seems to be a proclaimer of foreign gods.' (They said this because he was preaching the good news about Jesus and the resurrection.)" (v. 18).

- He used the novelty of his approach to his advantage. His audience asked: "'What is this new teaching? Can we learn what you are talking about? You've told us some strange things and we want to know what they mean.' (They said this because all Athenians as well as the foreigners who live in Athens used to spend their time doing nothing but talking about or listening to the newest thing.)" (vv. 19-21).

- Rather than berate them for idolatry, he approached them with respect: "Paul stood up in the middle of the council on Mars Hill and said, 'People of Athens, I see that you are very religious in every way'" (v. 22).

- Instead of starting with their differences, he spelled out the link between their spiritual practice and the way of Jesus Christ: "As I was walking through town and carefully observing your objects of worship, I even found an altar with this inscription: 'To an unknown God.' What you worship as unknown, I now proclaim to you. God, who made the world and everything in it, is Lord of heaven and earth. He doesn't live in temples made with human hands. Nor is God served by human hands, as though he needed something, since he is the one who gives life, breath, and everything else. From one person God created every human nation to live on the whole earth, having determined their appointed times and the boundaries of their lands. God made the nations so they would seek him, perhaps even reach out to him and find him" (vv. 23-27).

- And instead of starting with scripture, he cited their own philosophers and poets: "In fact, God isn't very far away from any of us. In God we live, move, and exist. As some of your own poets said, 'We are his offspring'" (vv. 27-28).

What a winsome approach! It is no wonder that "some people joined him and came to believe, including Dionysius, a member of the council on Mars Hill, a woman named Damaris, and several others" (v. 34).

Notice that while Paul reaches out whole-heartedly, he doesn't dilute his message to win numbers or reduce the gospel to the least common denominator or imply that everything the Greeks believed was fine. He was clear and differentiating. We see this same care in other places, like 1 Corinthians 1:18, when Paul reminds us that "the message of the cross is foolishness" to philosophers who seek wisdom as their esoteric calling; or 1 Corinthians 2:1, when Paul resists preaching "God's secrets" as if following Jesus were a mystery religion. Instead, the way of Jesus is distinctive. It aspires to hopefulness (Rom 8:18-25), authenticity (Rom 12:9-12), compassion (Phil 2:1-5), humility (Phil 2:5-11), and joy (Phil 4:4-8).

Finally, Paul and other Christian leaders were what we would call "media savvy." We're so used to reading "Paul's Letter to the Galatians" or "the Letter from James" that we neglect to appreciate the way the apostles availed themselves of the new media of letters carried swiftly across Roman roads. As Tom Standage titled his *Wired* e-magazine article: "Social Media? It's Not a New Idea. Try Following Cicero and Caesar's Feeds": "For the elite of the late Roman Republic in the first century, papyrus rolls carried by messengers served the same purpose as Twitter does today, allowing letters, news, speeches, essays and books to be shared and discussed." Here is an example from Cicero: "I sent you on March 24 a copy of Balbus's letter to me and of Caesar's letter to him," he wrote to a friend. Scribes and messengers copied and carried documents, from dashed-off notes to books. A single copy of the newspaper *Acta Diurna* was produced and posted at the Forum. Choosing, copying, and distributing the best bits was left to its readers.[6]

But Paul and other early Christian leaders did not just use the media tools for novelty's sake. They used them to build relationships: to maintain a conversation with believers and to deepen ties among members of the communities.

There's a lot we can learn from our culturally shrewd first-century counterparts. Let's explore how Paul's pre-Christendom approach can guide our way in our post-Christendom world.

Reaching Out to the Culture Today

Just as the early church learned how to become cultural interpreters to the world, we have that opportunity today. Not long ago, American congregations were in sync with the mainline culture. Now we live in an increasingly secular world. Depending on where you live on the post-Christendom continuum, the impact varies.

For some Christians, life is just a little more complicated as church priorities get pressed by competing expectations. Many parents in my church are caught between a rock and a hard place, wanting to get their kids to church when youth sports demand Sunday morning attendance.

For others, the shift is extraordinarily distressing: they feel under assault from the culture to conform. In some states, conservative Christians are fighting to keep their "moral majority" legislatively with laws restricting abortion or battling for "freedom of conscience" by reserving the right not to serve gays. They are grieving the religious preeminence that they assumed for generations.

The flip side is that Christians have opportunities to engage the culture in new ways. The choices we make, the places we go, the words we say, and the actions we take all testify to the name of Christ that we bear. Paul's model is a great place to start.

Taking the Gospel to the "Marketplace"

In too many places, we consider other churches our competition. What if we were less interested in stealing sheep from somebody else's pasture and instead followed Paul's cue to take the gospel to the marketplace? While it's important for us to continue to have interchurch conversations about the truth of the gospel, we're just shooting ourselves in the foot if that's all we do.

Where is today's marketplace in which people are talking about values and ideas? In some places, it's not very different from the ancient Agora in Athens. National Public Radio ran a story about one such spot in Southern California: "Stroll through the plaza of Balboa Park in San Diego, and you'll pass religious groups spreading their beliefs and looking for converts. But you'll also see a table draped with a large banner that reads, 'Relax, Hell Does Not Exist.'" It's run by the San Diego Coalition of Reason, one other option alongside Scientologists, Hare Krishnas, and a number of Christian organizations.[7]

This "on the ground" kind of conversation is increasingly important. There will always be places where dialogue and debate occur among religious leaders. The first World Parliament of Religions occurred in 1893 at the Chicago World's Fair; its centenary launched a series of conferences and a renewed commitment to cross-religious understanding.[8] But in a time of shifting authority, conversations among official leaders matter less and less.

The savviest enterprises are taking the interfaith conversation to the people. This was the goal of a video program I participated in called "One God," a conversation with Rabbi Sherre Hirsch and Muslim leader Eboo Patel.[9] Patel is taking it further still through Interfaith Youth Core, an organization that brings college students together to roll up their sleeves in service. "Until Mr. Patel came along," a *New York Times* article notes,

> the interfaith movement in the United States was largely the province of elders and clergy members hosting dialogues and, yes, book clubs—and drafting documents that had little impact at the grass roots. Meanwhile at the grass roots, inter-religious friction was sparking regularly over public school holidays, zoning permits for houses of worship and religious garb in the workplace.

As people of different faiths interact with increasing frequency, Patel's program seeks to create "positive, meaningful relationships across differences."[10]

More and more, ordinary Christians will be interacting with people of other faiths—and of no faith at all—in our workplaces, at school, and over coffee with friends. Rather than see this as a threat to our beliefs, it's an opportunity for us to *witness* to what we believe. Sometimes this happens in words, sometimes in deeds, and often in both. A member of my church takes his witness to the gospel to work, where he keeps his Bible on his desk. A small group of entrepreneurs is pursuing a "Faith and Leadership Initiative" to equip CEOs and young professionals to face ethical challenges. John Vest, previously quoted youth pastor at Fourth Presbyterian Church in downtown Chicago, takes the message of Christ to Bears' football games with a tailgate barbecue with the church's name front and center. Jen Hatmaker describes the witness their congregation in Austin, Texas, made:

> This year, Austin New Church decided to rethink "The Traditional Easter Service That Brings In More People Than Any Other Day of the Year." It is our church's two-year anniversary, and certainly we could stand more foot traffic, but I'm not sure [Easter] is best celebrated by a high-attendance Sunday of people who won't be back until Christmas Eve.
>
> We literally asked ourselves . . . What would Jesus do? Would He drop a bunch of cash on fancy clothes? Buy out the chocolate and plastic egg supply? Find the biggest church in town and spend twenty minutes posturing in the lobby?
>
> Who in Austin might want to celebrate the astonishing hope of resurrected Jesus but might feel uncomfortable surrounded by beautiful people dressed to the nines? Who needs the gospel spoke into their brokenness but might not be welcomed by the saints in the sanctuaries? It came quickly to us:
>
> The homeless.
>
> If Jesus came to proclaim freedom for the captives and good news to the poor, then [Easter] uniquely belongs to the bottom dwellers. So we cancelled service and took church downtown to the corner of 7th and Neches, where our homeless community is concentrated. We grilled thirteen hundred burgers and ate together. Our band led worship; then in a powerful moment of solidarity, we shared Communion. It was a beautiful mess of

dancing, tears, singing, and sharing. It wasn't an *us* and *them* moment; it was just the church, remembering the Passover Lamb and celebrating our liberation together.[11]

That's an amazing example of taking the gospel to the public square.

Another creative idea comes from Jan Edmiston, associate executive in Chicago Presbytery. She suggests that our traditional model of church planting needs updating. For years, mainline denominations have turned to three models: the "Parachute Drop Model," in which an entrepreneurial pastor is dropped into a new subdivision; the "Established-Church-Sending-People-to-Start-Something-on-the-Other-End-of-the-County Model," encouraging current members who live ten miles from church to start their own branch; and the "Immigrant Start-Up Meeting in an Established Church's Building," where two congregations share space together. The problem is that the first two models have ceased being effective, and the third runs the risk of the "established" church treating the immigrant congregation less as a partner than a tenant to help with the bills. Instead of traditional churches with buildings, Edmiston suggests, "we need communities of faith for those who are spiritually curious, who would never 'go to church' in a traditional setting."

Instead, she proposes that established churches call "neighborhood pastors." She imagines a paradigm shift. Instead of calling a traditional associate pastor for internal programs, the neighborhood pastor would serve outside the church. Instead of keeping an office inside the church, the pastor would hold conversations at coffee shops and in the park. Instead of seeking to minister internally to church members, the pastor would seek out school counselors, community leaders, and health professionals to support their work and discern what the neighborhood needs. Instead of worrying over what potential members might have to offer to the church, the pastor would help the church discern "what breaks God's heart" in the neighborhood, and how the church could offer support and ministries.

Edmiston recognizes that members might balk, asking questions like:

> Why are we paying for an Associate Pastor who's not serving *us* and *our* needs? . . . What if these people never "join" and help contribute financially?[12]

Indeed, both Jan Edmiston's and Jen Hatmaker's proposals may sound absurd to our ears, attuned to the traditional tune of doing church. But to the ears of the early Christians, it would sound strikingly familiar.

Engaging with the Culture: Language, Respect, and Links

But being *in* the community is just the first step. Next, the Apostle Paul used the language of the culture rather than Jewish religious terms. He didn't just use their ideas; he approached them with respect. And, instead of starting with their differences, he spelled out the link between their spiritual practice and the way of Jesus Christ, even citing their own philosophers and poets.

What would that mean for us? Just as Paul borrowed language from Epicurean and Stoic philosophers, we need to translate the gospel into today's vernacular, including the languages of other religions, if need be. When we use their languages, it's not to tear them down, but to understand them and even see the overlaps among the different religions.

That doesn't mean we compromise our values or dilute our beliefs. Instead, the clearer we are about what is central to us and what is indifferent—what is *esse* and what is *adiaphora*—the more nimble we can be about conveying the core message of the gospel in cross-cultural ways. And the more we know about other religious options, the greater clarity and confidence we have about places of overlap and places of difference.

For example, many Americans (especially people who enjoy yoga) have been attracted to Buddhism. Instead of being afraid of Buddhism as a foreign cult, we can lift up places where Christianity offers similar teaching. Jesus says, "Do not store up for yourselves treasures on earth, where moth and rust consume and where thieves break in and steal; but store up for yourselves treasures in heaven, where neither moth nor rust consumes and where thieves do not break in and steal. For where your treasure is, there your heart will be also" (Matt 6:19-21 NRSV). We can relate his words to the Buddhists' idea of "detachment." Jesus says, "The eye is the lamp of the body. So, if your eye is healthy, your whole body will be full of light; but if your eye is unhealthy, your whole body will be full of darkness. If then the light in you is darkness, how great is the darkness!" (Matt 6:22-23 NRSV); and

> Do not judge, so that you may not be judged. For with the judgment you make you will be judged, and the measure you give will be the measure you get. Why do you see the speck in your neighbor's eye, but do not notice the log in your own eye? Or how can you say to your neighbor, "Let me take the speck out of your eye," while the log is in your own eye? You hypocrite, first take the log out of your own eye, and then you will see clearly to take the speck out of your neighbor's eye. (Matt 7:1-5 NRSV)

We can point out similarities between Jesus's words and those of Bodhidharma (ca. 440–528 CE):

> Unless you see your nature, you shouldn't go around criticizing the goodness of others. There's no advantage in deceiving yourself. Good and bad are distinct. Cause and effect are clear. But fools don't believe and fall straight into a hell of endless darkness without even knowing it. What keeps them from believing is the heaviness of their karma. They're like blind people who don't believe there's such a thing as light. Even if you explain it to them, they still don't believe, because they're blind. How can they possibly distinguish light?[13]

Are there differences? Absolutely. But Paul didn't start with differences, and if we want to reach the culture, then neither should we.

An Undiluted—but Winsome—Message

Yet, just like Paul, there is no need to dilute the message to win numbers or reduce the gospel to the least common denominator or imply that everything the culture believes is fine. While it can be tempting to smooth over differences with an adage like "All roads lead up the same mountain," we do not honor others by pretending we all believe the same thing. So, for example, in contrast with Buddhism, Christians do not believe suffering is caused by "karma"—"the force created by a person's actions that some people believe causes good or bad things to happen to that person."[14] Instead, we believe that sin and evil are at work in the world, and Jesus has come alongside us to break their power through the strength of love. We trust Jesus when he says,

> You have heard that it was said, "You shall love your neighbor and hate your enemy." But I say to you, Love your enemies and pray for those who persecute you so that you may be children of your Father in heaven; for he makes his sun rise on the evil and on the good and sends rain on the righteous and on the unrighteous. (Matt 5:43-45)

What a different approach this is to the image that Christians too often present to the world. Nearly twenty years ago, I was living in Portland, Oregon. Even then, Oregon was already one of the most post-Christendom states in the country. Church attendance was very low, and the attitude of many Oregonians toward church was neutral at best and derisive at worst. But sometimes, the behavior of Christians did not help matters. I still vividly remember an experience I had shopping at an outlet mall in Lincoln City. As I was leafing through a rack of sweaters at a clothing store, two women were loudly talking with each other. One said, "It's too bad my neighbor doesn't believe in Jesus Christ. I just know she's going to hell." The other agreed, "Those poor people. They are just so ignorant and stupid." And I thought to myself, *And* that's *going to win people to Christ?* For many decades, comments like that wouldn't have mattered. But in a post-Christendom world, we can't afford for Christians to give Christ a bad name. Everything we do or say needs to reflect the love of God in Jesus Christ.

Media Savvy, Relationship Focused

Being culturally attuned is crucial. And part of that means being media savvy. Being media savvy isn't a gimmick. It's a way to get the message of the gospel across in fresh ways using the novelty of the message as an advantage.

One of the best examples of this is Pope Francis's winsome opening. Elected in March 2013, in the first year of his papacy, he had already used myriad forms of communication. Some of them were traditional, like conferences and encyclicals. He addressed the World Youth Day in Rio, saying: "Sharing the experience of faith, bearing witness to the faith, proclaiming the Gospel: this is a command that the Lord entrusts to the whole Church, and that includes you. . . . [Jesus] gave his life in order to save us and to show us the love and mercy of God."[15] A few months later, he issued a papal encyclical on poverty that contrasted "the joy of the gospel" with "the new idolatry of money": "In this system, which tends to devour everything which stands in the way of increased profits, whatever is fragile, like the environment, is defenseless before the interests of a deified market, which become the only rule."[16]

And Pope Francis also uses Facebook and Twitter, updating them regularly. @Pontifex includes Tweets like: "All of us who are baptized are missionary disciples. We are called to become a living Gospel in the world"; and, "The world makes us look towards ourselves, our possessions, our desires. The Gospel invites us to be open to others, to share with the poor."[17]

But, as NBC News noted, "more often than not, when asked which of Francis's comments this year resonated most with them, Catholics immediately mentioned his gestures, not his quotes:

Riding the bus back to the guest house after being named pope. Washing the feet of prisoners on Holy Thursday. Turning an '84 Renault into the Popemobile. Celebrating his birthday with the homeless. Embracing a disfigured fan. Cold-calling people who write to him.[18]

93

No wonder he's *Time*'s "Person of the Year," is Twitter's #bestpopeever, and even made the cover of *Rolling Stone* magazine.[19] People *want* to belong to a community marked by such service and love.

But even without the fan base the pope has, we can become more media savvy. In fact, we *need* to be. Pastor Carey Nieuwhof reminds us that it was not that long ago that to hear great preaching or music required showing up in person. Now, podcasting and online campuses, YouTube and iPods have changed everything.

Nieuwhof, whose primary mission is to reach the unchurched, suggests media presence that does not just get messages out but also encourages community. People are connecting with one another in ways they never have before, through Twitter and Facebook, websites and blogs, podcasts and apps. For those of us in traditional congregations, he urges, "Don't judge your people for not being there, help them stay connected instead."[20]

But Nieuwhof, like the Apostle Paul, understands that the goal of media is not just to get the message out but also to help build up the church.

So he urges us to create irresistible experiences that people miss if they are not there. Just as a performance on YouTube cannot compete with a live concert, an online church experience is not the same as worship in person; and just as a Skype chat cannot compare with a flesh-and-blood visit, e-church cannot substitute for a hallway hug or a place at the Lord's Table. Nieuwhof suggests fun activities—in the foyer, parking lot, or service—that are not podcasted. One of their not-to-be-missed moments included sharing beloved Canadian treats (gourmet butter tarts) with everyone who showed up on a long weekend. Needless to say, those who were not there are on the lookout for the next adventure.

Novelty in itself is not the point; it is the hunger people have not to miss out on community, joy, and surprise. And even more, people do not want to miss out on the opportunity for meaning and service in life. But that is just the beginning of their engagement, not the end. Nieuwhof urges us:

> Create a culture of serving. . . . When you get up early to set up and tear
> down, lead a 2nd grade small group, greet people with a smile, serve on the

production team, or serve meals to the homeless, somehow you find a place in service of a goal greater than yourself.[21]

The gospel holds a powerful attraction for those who are hungry for their lives to matter.

Choosing Christ in an Age of Endless Choices

The days when everyone in the West belonged to a church because they were "supposed to" are long gone. Once, children might have grown up going to their parents' church and stayed with the denomination because they were expected to be loyal to their family's "brand." But now that individuals are offered countless choices in every aspect of our lives, should it surprise us that brand loyalty is a thing of the past?

We have become a consumer-driven, choice-based culture. We face more choices than any generation in human history. Before we even head out the door, we've chosen the soap for our bodies and clothes for our backs; coffee or tea to clear our heads and breakfast to fill our stomachs. And to fill our heads? We choose from news on TV or in the paper; e-mails or texts; electronic games or crossword puzzles. Some studies show that by the end of the day we're faced with as many as thirty-five thousand choices. For those of us who start our day at a coffee shop, there may be more. Diana Butler Bass reports a conversation she once had with a coffee executive. She asked him how many choices were available to his customers. He told her that in drink items alone there were eighty-two thousand options on the menu.[22] Business schools have a name for today's tyranny of choices: they call it "decision fatigue."[23]

The cultural norm of obligation is over, replaced by the culture of choice. For decades, leaders in American churches fought it. We tried to make people feel guilty for not coming to church, but it didn't work. Now there are only vestiges of religious obligation left: religious weddings and funerals, having your baby baptized, and attending worship on Christmas and Easter. Someday those too will likely fade, as they have already in Europe and the most secular corners of America.

We cannot make the culture feel religiously obligated. Instead, we're back to where we started, two thousand years ago, before Christendom, when the religious marketplace was almost as varied as a coffee shop is today. Now Christians have opportunities to engage the culture in new ways—both winsome and prophetic—without compromising the core of our faith. And instead of people participating because they're supposed to, they come because they're engaged. What a privilege to share the message of Jesus Christ!

Depending on where we live, we will find ourselves in different places on the post-Christendom continuum. But wherever we find ourselves, we have the opportunity to take the good news into the world. Our marketplace might be the streets where the homeless live, the bar on the corner, the boardroom at the office, or the clothing store at the outlet mall. Our culture's language might be that of new immigrants in our changing neighborhoods, our kids' football or baseball teams, a business round table focused on success, or the PTA meeting. Respecting and connecting with the spiritual practices of non-Christians might mean taking yoga classes at the gym, discussing business ethics at a conference, exploring fellow volunteers' motivation for compassion at a blood drive or soup kitchen, or taking a seminar in world religions. Being media savvy may include posting a word about faith on Facebook, joining a progressive political cause where Christians are less visible, wearing a cross necklace or getting a tattoo, speaking up—winsomely—for Christ in class or at the local tavern. Being relationally focused may inspire us to show up more often to teach Sunday school or tutor in the slums, visit a sick member in the hospital or a stranger in prison, build houses for the homeless or get involved in a cause for justice.

None of this means diluting our message. In fact, just the opposite! It requires us to be crystal clear about what is truly important in our faith and to carry that message in all that we say and do, including how we treat each other.

Chapter 6

Can't We All Just Get Along?

Fight Erupts in Jerusalem Church," was the lead in the BBC news:

> Israeli police had to break up a fist fight that erupted between Greek and Ar-
> menian Orthodox clergymen at one of Christianity's holiest sites. The scuffles
> broke out at the Church of the Holy Sepulchre in Jerusalem on Orthodox
> Palm Sunday. Brawls are not uncommon at the church, which is uneasily
> shared by various Christian denominations. . . . Witnesses say an Armenian
> priest forcibly ejected a Greek priest from an area near the tomb of Jesus . . .
> [for spending] too long at the tomb. When police arrived to break up the
> fight, some were reportedly beaten back by worshippers using palm fronds.[1]

What a remarkable image: waving Palm Sunday fronds not to proclaim the
message of Christ but to beat people over the head.

But church fights are hardly uncommon in the United States. "An Unforgiving Power Struggle at a Los Feliz Church," read the headline in the *Los
Angeles Times*, describing a fight at St. Mary of the Angels, an Anglican parish
"embroiled in an odd sort of holy war." A number of people were taking the
lead of their pastor, Reverend Kelley, who was seeking to lead the parish to

---

This chapter title comes from Rodney King in his response to the Los Angeles riots erupting
in 1992. The riots blew up after he was brutally beaten by police, the incident was caught on
tape, and the officers who beat him were acquitted.

join the Roman Catholic Church. On the other side were church members and Anglican leaders who "accused Kelley of wrongdoing, took him to court, ran him out of the church and changed the locks. Church quarrels are frequently decided in courtrooms, particularly when property is involved. . . . But the St. Mary's saga is notable for its viciousness. The church has perhaps 60 members, and the bickering among them has been marked by incendiary accusations and screaming matches that often end with 'God is on our side!'"[2]

"TBN Embroiled in 'Sordid' Family Lawsuit," posted the headline in *Christianity Today*:

> The granddaughter of Trinity Broadcasting Network founders Paul and Jan Crouch has accused some of the network's directors of illegally distributing "charitable assets" worth more than $50 million for their personal use. Brittany B. Koper, the daughter of Paul Crouch Jr., was TBN's chief financial officer until last September. She says she was wrongfully fired after she refused to cover up the alleged distribution scheme.[3]

Sadly, internecine warfare is not uncommon in churches. Mainline and Roman Catholic, Evangelical and Eastern Orthodox: no strand of Christianity is exempt from church fights. But as this small sample of headlines makes clear, these wars do more than harm the internal well-being of the body of Christ. They also give the church a black eye in the public arena.

Public perception of Christian fights isn't a new problem, of course. But it's urgently important now in our post-Christendom era, when people don't automatically seek the church. How we behave with each other is crucial, especially in our witness to the next generation. In research involving 1,200 American "millennials" (those born between 1980 and 2000), Thom and Jess Rainer outline just how critical this issue is for young adults:

> "I went to a business meeting at that church. I'm never going back." His name is Kevin. He is a 29-year-old man from Kentucky. Kevin, by his own

admission, is not a Christian. "Something made me visit that church," he told me. "I'm not sure what it was, but I know now it was a big mistake."

Kevin told me how he one day on a whim decided to go to a business meeting in the church he had visited for four weeks. He also told me how he was "blown away" by the petty disagreements and harsh language in the meeting. He was saddened to listen to one man speak in deep anger to someone else. That man was his small group leader.

"I felt like I was at a playground fight with six-year olds. Boy did I make a mistake visiting a church."

We are losing Kevin's generation. Over eighty-two million in number (greater even than the seventy-seven million baby boomers[4]), they are the fastest-growing quadrant of the "nones"—those with "no religious affiliation." They are not so much rejecting Christianity as a way of life; they are rejecting churches as a place where they can grow spiritually, as the Rainers' research suggests:

Many of them are walking away from our churches, and more of them are not attending at all, when they witness or hear about negativity and divisiveness in those churches. They want to see unity among Christians, and they are often disappointed.

It's not that this generation wanted an "anything goes" church. In fact, they were attracted to congregations that were true to their core convictions. One typical response was from a young woman named Rebecca: "I would not expect a church to compromise its beliefs to accommodate me. To be honest, I am intrigued by their beliefs, and that's one of the reasons I'm visiting the church." Thom Rainer writes:

The issue for the Millennials was not an expectation of Christians and churches to compromise their doctrine. They simply are attracted to Christians and churches where unity is real and evident. For almost all of the Millennials in our study, 97 percent to be precise, mutual respect was a critical issue in any relationship. And 64 percent of them expressed these feelings strongly, higher than all the other attitudes we measured.

It seems, therefore, that Christians and churches will win the right to be heard by Millennials when those Christians and churches demonstrate love and unity among themselves. And the early reporting from the Millennial generation about this issue is not too encouraging. We Christians and the churches we represent may be one of the biggest stumbling blocks to reaching the largest generation in America's history.[5]

How do we learn to behave better *within* the church—not just to "play nice" or be healthy, but for the cause of our witness to the world? It isn't easy! But we're hardly the first to engage in this struggle. Even though the early Christians didn't have twenty-four-hour headline news to contend with, word got around fast in their new world of paved roads, parchment, and papyrus. What might happen if we cleared the fog of cryptomnesia and re-membered what we learned before?

Early Christians, Early Fights

Our current struggles abound. Social issues like same-sex marriage and abortion. Authority issues like women's leadership and LGBTQ ordination. Financial issues like property and pensions. Internal issues like buildings and music. These particular issues are unique to our time. Yet I'm amazed at how similar our struggles are to the problems confronting the early church! In addition to the questions about the faith they inherited—what was crucial to keep (*esse*), and what could go either way (*adiaphora*)—there were plenty of other arguments and choices the first believers had to wrestle through in their day-to-day lives.

There were *social issues*: how to navigate cultural norms like food offered to idols and societal customs dividing slave and free, male and female, Jew and Greek. There were *issues of authority*: what pieces of the Jewish law to honor, whether women could speak in the church, how to resolve conflicting opinions among apostles and teachers, and how much hierarchy was helpful.

There were *financial issues*: what monetary support was due church leaders, how much to share resources, and how to ensure equitable care for the poor in different communities. And then there were *internal issues*: fights among members within particular communities over all of the above, plus everything else that makes us human.

Scripture isn't shy about recording church conflict in our early years. Paul refers to fights in almost every letter. Here are just a few of the conflicts he addresses.

In Philippi:

> I urge Euodia and I urge Syntyche to come to an agreement in the Lord. Yes, and I'm also asking you, loyal friend, to help these women who have struggled together with me in the ministry of the gospel. (Phil 4:2-3)

In Galatia:

> I'm amazed that you are so quickly deserting the one who called you by the grace of Christ to follow another gospel. It's not really another gospel, but certain people are confusing you and they want to change the gospel of Christ. (Gal 1:6-8)

In Rome:

> Welcome the person who is weak in faith—but not in order to argue about differences of opinion. One person believes in eating everything, while the weak person eats only vegetables. Those who eat must not look down on the ones who don't, and the ones who don't eat must not judge the ones who do, because God has accepted them. (Rom 14:1-3)

It wasn't just in the Pauline churches either! We find similar admonitions in the Letter of James:

> What is the source of conflict among you? What is the source of your disputes? Don't they come from your cravings that are at war in your own lives?

You long for something you don't have, so you commit murder. You are jealous for something you can't get, so you struggle and fight. (4:1-2)

Conflict didn't stop when the New Testament was completed either. As we know, the battles continued among the early believers. Bishop Ignatius of Antioch (ca. 50–117 CE) wrote to the church at Smyrna:

> Let not place puff any one up: for that which is worth all is a faith and love, to which nothing is to be preferred. But consider those who are of a different opinion with respect to the grace of Christ which has come unto us, how opposed they are to the will of God. They have no regard for love; no care for the widow, or the orphan, or the oppressed; of the bond, or of the free; of the hungry, or of the thirsty.[6]

For the early church, life together wasn't "sweetness and light." These weren't easy times.

So how did they do it? In light of their real conflicts and differences within the churches and the plethora of attractive options across the Empire, how did they find a way forward? It started with the conviction that their calling was of higher value than their differences, as Paul reminds the church in Ephesus:

> Therefore, as a prisoner for the Lord, I encourage you to live as people worthy of the call you received from God. Conduct yourselves with all humility, gentleness, and patience. Accept each other with love, and make an effort to preserve the unity of the Spirit with the peace that ties you together. You are one body and one spirit, just as God also called you to one hope. There is one Lord, one faith, one baptism, and one God and Father of all, who is over all, through all, and in all. (Eph 4:1-5)

We've already reviewed in detail some of the first steps they took to "preserve the unity of the Spirit" that held them together:

- They *shared a commitment to the essentials*: following the way of Jesus Christ and sincerely desiring that the fruit of the Holy Spirit be made manifest in and through them. They focused on "one Lord, one faith, one baptism, one God and Father of all" (Eph 4:5), rather than allowing themselves to be distracted by the endless number of points on which they might disagree.

- They acknowledged that *some things were adiaphora—indifferent things*—and those things might be murky and changing. Paul even disagrees with himself at times! When addressing the issue of women speaking in church, he first instructs women who pray or prophesy in church to wear veils (1 Cor 11:5); but three chapters later, Paul tells women to be silent, since they've been dominating worship (1 Cor 14:34).

- They *came together to discern*: they took turns testifying and listening to each other's witness. They recognized that no single voice could speak for God, and they needed each other: "The apostles and the elders gathered to consider the matter" (Acts 15:6). Practicing empathy wasn't easy, but the more they heard each other, the more they trusted the decisions that were made.

- They *sought the upbuilding of the whole household* with genuine affection. The gifts they enjoyed were considered not prizes to be hoarded but resources to be offered for the well-being of Christ's family. As Paul wrote, "If there is any encouragement in Christ, any comfort in love, any sharing in the Spirit, any sympathy, complete my joy by thinking the same way, having the same love, being united, and agreeing with each other. Don't do anything for selfish purposes, but with humility think of others as better than yourselves. Instead of each person watching out for their own good, watch out for what is better for others" (Phil 2:1-4). Why? Because this was "the attitude that was in Christ Jesus" (Phil 2:5): the one who invited us to be family (Mark 3:34-35; Luke 8:21); the one who taught us how to love God and neighbor (e.g., Luke 10:27); the one who gave us "a new commandment": "Love each other. Just as I have loved you, so you also must love each other. This is how everyone will know that you are my disciples, when you love each other" (John 13:34-35).

This, above all, is why the early Christians worked so hard at loving each other in community. It wasn't to be nice or politically correct or to have a united front against the rest of the culture. It wasn't even to look good to the outside world, as if appearances were the point. How they treated each other was *at the core of who they were as followers of Jesus.* They needed to be enacting that which they were professing. If they weren't, it was all a sham. If they didn't embody his love, how could they bear his name?

Paul captures this urgency in his letter to the feuding believers in Corinth:

> If anyone is in Christ, that person is part of the new creation. The old things have gone away, and look, new things have arrived! All these new things are from God, who reconciled us to himself through Christ and who gave us the ministry of reconciliation. In other words, God was reconciling the world to himself through Christ, by not counting people's sins against them. He has trusted us with this message of reconciliation. So we are ambassadors who represent Christ. (2 Cor 5:17-20)

Doing the "ministry of reconciliation" isn't an add-on to being a Christian. It is *at the center of what it means to follow Christ.* It takes practice. And there are a number of specific steps the apostles provide us:

First, *don't be naïve.* Sin is at work in the world, and to pretend otherwise would set us up for failure. In Paul's second letter to Timothy he writes of the days to come—not just in the world, but also in the life of the church:

> People will be selfish and love money. They will be the kind of people who brag and who are proud. They will slander others, and they will be disobedient to their parents. They will be ungrateful, unholy, unloving, contrary, and critical. They will be without self-control and brutal, and they won't love what is good. They will be people who are disloyal, reckless, and conceited. They will love pleasure instead of loving God. They will look like they are religious but deny God's power. (2 Tim 3:2-5)

Second, *call each other to account but recognize your own faults first.* "If a person is caught doing something wrong"—and, as we've seen, they will!—"you who are spiritual should restore someone like this *with a spirit of gentleness.* Watch out for yourselves so you won't be tempted too. Carry each other's burdens and so you will fulfill the law of Christ. . . . Each person should test their own work" (Gal 6:1-4, emphasis mine).

The early Christians recognized that part of the very sin that Jesus died to overcome is our tendency to judge each other. Paul's admonition to speak "the truth with love" (Eph 4:15) is laid out with even greater specificity in James's word:

> Brothers and sisters, don't say evil things about each other. Whoever insults or criticizes a brother or sister insults and criticizes the Law. If you find fault with the Law, you are not a doer of the Law but a judge over it. There is only one lawgiver and judge, and he is able to save and to destroy. But you who judge your neighbor, who are you? (4:11-12)

Third, *continually strive for spiritual maturity*, or sanctification, in yourself, which is a lifelong lesson in humility and correction. The gifts of the Spirit don't appear all at once, but emerge in a believer's lifelong process of growing up. All of the Spirit's gifts—divided in countless different ways among various people—move toward the same end:

> To equip God's people for the work of serving and building up the body of Christ until we all reach the unity of faith and knowledge of God's Son. God's goal is for us to become mature adults—to be fully grown, measured by the standard of the fullness of Christ. . . . By speaking the truth with love, let's grow in every way into Christ, who is the head. . . . The body makes itself grow in that it builds itself up with love as each one does their part. (Eph 4:12-16)

Fourth, *when (not if!) there's conflict, work it out privately*, and, if at possible, continue to have mutual respect. Jesus gives clear instructions about keeping family business private:

If your brother or sister sins against you, go and correct them when you are alone together. If they listen to you, then you've won over your brother or sister. But if they won't listen, take with you one or two others so that *every word may be established by the mouth of two or three witnesses.* (Matt 18:15-16)

As we saw earlier, this instruction becomes a defined feature of conflict resolution in the early church (2 Cor 13:1, emphasis mine; cf. also Deut 19:5).

But sometimes, even the most faithful Christians could not stay together. They agreed on the essentials, they acknowledged their differences of non-essentials, they came together to discern, and they sought the upbuilding of the household of God. They weren't naïve; they recognized sin, calling each other to account and at the same time, recognizing their own faults. They strove for spiritual maturity in their own hearts, and when there was conflict, they sought to work it out privately. In the very rare event that there were genuine heretics—who, for example, denied Jesus as Lord—then they could dismiss them, treating them "as you would a Gentile and tax collector" (Matt 18:17). And still, there were conflicts among faithful Christians that couldn't be resolved by their staying together.

So they determined *as a last resort to go their separate ways to maintain the unity of Christ*. It wasn't always pretty, as we discover with Paul and Barnabas. Who was Barnabas? A Levite from Cyprus, the apostles gave him the name Barnabas, "son of encouragement," in part for his all-in generosity (Acts 4:36, NRSV). In many ways, Paul (aka Saul) would not have come to be part of Christ's family if not for Barnabas's intervention. When Saul was converted on the road to Damascus after having mercilessly persecuted the followers of Jesus, it was Barnabas who stood up for him: "Barnabas brought Saul to the apostles and told them the story about how Saul saw the Lord on the way and that the Lord had spoken to Saul. He also told them about the confidence with which Saul had preached in the name of Jesus in Damascus" (Acts 9:27).

Paul and Barnabas became the closest working partners, even refusing to receive payment for their apostolic services (1 Cor 9:6). First they served side by side in Antioch along with Simeon, Lucius, and Manaen (Acts 11:25-26; 13:1). Then they labored together in Seleucia and Cyprus, Iconium and Lystra, Pamphylia, Perga, and Attalia (Acts 13:2-5; 14:1-18, 24-25).

Yet, even after all they had been through together, there came an irreconcilable difference. The book of Acts reports their disagreement over John Mark. For a time, John had joined them. But then, when they got to Pamphylia, John ditched them and returned to the leaders in Jerusalem (13:13). Paul never trusted him again. Later, when Barnabas wanted to bring John Mark along on a mission with Paul, "the disagreement became so sharp that [Paul and Barnabas] parted company" (Acts 15:39, NRSV). Paul's letter to the Galatians reports that Barnabas "got carried away with them in their hypocrisy" (2:13). Paul was angry with Barnabas as well as Peter for siding with James on issues of purity. He felt that the Council at Jerusalem had settled once and for all that circumcision and eating meat offered to idols were *adiaphora*, and he resented the reopening of these issues yet again. So Paul and Barnabas split. Barnabas took John Mark to Cyprus, and Paul chose Silas to go with him to visit the churches in Syria and Cilicia (Acts 15:39-41).

Nevertheless, in spite of their disagreements, frustration, disappointment, and even feelings of betrayal, *the apostles sought to honor each other's ministry going forward. As long as they agreed on the essential of the lordship of Jesus*, early Christians put aside their significant differences for the sake of the unity of the gospel. They put aside differences regarding the Law and grace, differences over authority, and differences about moral issues like marrying nonbelievers and eating meat offered to idols.

When they went their separate ways, they went to reach out to the culture where they best fit: Paul and Silas to some; Barnabas and John Mark to others; James and Peter to others still. Rather than compete against each other, they competed against other options in the Greco-Roman mission field. As long as they kept faithful to what was central, they honored each other, because the good news of the gospel was essential—far more essential than their differences.

Why did it matter so much? Because part of their *central* identity as followers of Jesus was to be *agents of reconciliation* in his name and because the fruit of the Spirit was, above all, love (1 Cor 13). Love for God, one another, and neighbor was the identifying mark above all others for followers of Jesus.

And the Roman Empire took note.[7] Justin Martyr (ca. 100–165 CE) sketched the impact of Christian love this way: "We who used to value the acquisition of wealth and possessions more than anything else now bring what we have into a common fund and share it with anyone who needs it. We used to hate and destroy one another and refused to associate with people of another race or country. Now, because of Christ, we live together with such people and pray for our enemies."[8]

Clement of Alexandra (ca. 150–215 CE) described the impact of the believers' love this way:

> He impoverishes himself, in order that he may never overlook a brother who has been brought into affliction, through the perfection that is in love, especially if he know[s] that he will bear want himself easier than his brother. He considers, accordingly, the other's pain his own grief; and if, by contributing from his own indigence in order to do good, he suffer any hardship, he does not fret at this, but augments his beneficence still more. For he possesses in its sincerity the faith which is exercised in reference to the affairs of life, and praises the Gospel in practice and contemplation. And, in truth, he wins his praise "not from men, but from God," by the performance of what the Lord has taught.[9]

By the third century, this central Christian trait of love was embedded as the core mark of their life together. The writer Tertullian (ca. 150–220 CE) noted that even pagans who were embroiled in conflict were impressed by the reputation of the Christians: "See how much they love each other."[10]

Managing Our Conflict Today

When asked to identify the main problem in the Western church, N. T. Wright names "the scandal of disunity." Imagining the reaction of Jesus or the earliest apostles to the church today, he suspects they would say: "We just can't believe how you have all of these different Christian movements and often they hardly even talk to each other or they're very suspicious of each other." This isn't new. Of course it was a problem for the first Christians too. Wright acknowledges how hard Paul had to work to get the various house churches in Rome to get to know each other, overcome suspicion, and appreciate their differences, so that, in Paul's words, "you can glorify the God and Father of our Lord Jesus Christ together with one voice" (Rom 15:6). But like the early Christians, Wright says,

> we've all colluded in the scandal of disunity, which is one of the reasons why much of the world doesn't take the church terribly seriously. . . .
>
> Every single letter Paul writes has a major emphasis on the unity of the church. He knew it was difficult, we know it's difficult, but that's no excuse. He was addressing it, and so should we.[11]

Conflict happens. In and of itself, it's not a bad thing. Sometimes through conflict, truth is revealed, ideas are honed, direction is discerned. But *how* we address conflict is as crucial today as it was in the early church.

As we wrestle with social issues, disagreements over authority, financial disputes, and internal divisions, we have the opportunity to live out our central calling to love one another as Christ has loved us. And the better we get at it, the stronger our witness to the world will be.

There isn't a congregation or assembly, district or presbytery that is devoid of conflict. The names have changed, but the early Christians' disagreements could be our own. Just as Paul urged Euodia and Syntyche to "come to an agreement in the Lord" (Phil 4:2), pastors today are urging Edith and Sue or Ed and Stan to do the same. Just as Paul despaired over flighty congregants "deserting the one who called you" (Gal 1:6), bishops and executive presbyters despair over congregations splitting over leadership. Just as Paul tired of members arguing over "differences of opinion" (Rom 14:1)—even major ones—leaders today tire of members sitting in judgment of each other. And just as James warned his people that their disputes weren't noble, but evidence of their jealousy (Jas 4:2), advisors today warn congregations that their struggles are killing them.

But beyond the wise warnings of the apostles, we can also learn from their actions, starting with the conviction that our sacred calling is far more precious than the differences that trouble us. To the extent that we:

"live as people worthy of the call you received from God" (Eph 4:1);

"conduct yourselves with all humility, gentleness, and patience"
(Eph 4:2);

"accept each other with love" (Eph 4:2); and

"make an effort to preserve the unity of the Spirit with the peace that ties you together" (Eph 4:3).

Then we will evidence that which we proclaim:

[We] are one body and one spirit, just as God also called [us] in one hope. There is one Lord, one faith, one baptism, and one God and Father of all, who is over all, through all, and in all. (Eph 4:4-5)

The steps we have in front of us are clear:

- To share *publicly* our commitment to the central core of faith in Jesus Christ rather than allow ourselves to be distracted by the endless number of points on which we genuinely disagree. In an era in which the media are attracted to bad news like bees to honey (or flies to rubbish!), we need to be very clear and very public about our unity in Christ. Like the early church, we need to broadcast our commitment to "one Lord, one faith, one baptism, one God and Father of all" (Eph 4:5) with far more volume than we whisper our differences. An extension of being media savvy (see chapter 5), we need to do a much better job of keeping our arguments private and our unity public.

- To <u>acknowledge among ourselves that some things—probably a *lot* of things!—are *adiaphora*</u>—indifferent things. We also need to recognize that what is considered *adiaphora* will change over time, just as it did in the early church. What once was "obviously" wrong isn't always. That was true among the first Christians when they changed their minds about meat offered to idols and circumcision. It has been true among American Christians too, as we have changed our minds about abolitionism, divorce, and, in some places, women in leadership. We will change our minds again. That does not mean we are unfaithful or shallow. It means we are "majoring in the majors" and letting some things go, even when we deeply disagree.

- To <u>come together to discern, taking turns testifying and listening</u>. It is easy to get tired of endless meetings going over the same matter again and again. And honestly, if all we do is listen to ourselves talk while we convince ourselves of our righteousness, it is pointless. Only when we are willing to presume that the other Christian *might* be speaking with the authority of the Spirit do we have a prayer of allowing discernment to happen. Practicing this intellectual empathy will not be easy, but it is crucial that we recognize that we need each other. It is also critical that we practice humility about our own convictions. I will never forget the witness of one of my colleagues in the Chicago Presbytery in our denomination's decades-long battle over gay ordination. Dave Handley, then pastor of First Presbyterian Church in Evanston, gave an impassioned and thoughtful testimony in favor of strict ordination standards. But he ended his speech with these words: "Then again, I might be wrong." That one sentence did more to build trust in the church than a million arguments combined.

- To <u>build up the whole household with affection</u>. One of the assumptions of our culture is a "winner-take-all" rule of life. It is pervasive, showing up in sports, business, government, school, video games, and cooking shows. It even infects the church. But the Kingdom offers an alternative to this zero-sum game, in which one wins and another loses, or one gains at the expense of another. We witness to the Spirit's alternative math: that God's gifts do not subtract from or compete with each other. Instead, they multiply and magnify each other. Like an orchestra or band whose voices each contribute, the whole becomes greater than the sum of its parts. This is the algorithm of Christ, whose new commandment—*"Just as I have loved you, so you also must love each other"*—shows us the "even better way" of love (John 13:34; 1 Cor 12:31).

If loving one another is at the core of our identity as followers of Jesus, then what will it look like? How do we enact this gospel we profess? How do we embody the name of Christ today? How do we honor, in the words of Paul, "the ministry of reconciliation" entrusted to us as ambassadors of Christ (2 Cor 5:17-20)? We start by taking up the practices we learned in our earliest days as Christ's followers:

<u>First, we cannot be naïve.</u> Denial is not helpful. In fact, we get into some of our deepest trouble when we pretend everything is fine when it's not. Clergy misconduct, whether financial or sexual, is often the result of keeping up appearances when life is falling apart. Awareness of temptation, compassion for the broken, and honesty about weakness are all crucial for the health of Christ's family.

And sin is always ready to pounce! We know all too well the reality of Paul's words to Timothy in our churches still, and it isn't OK. Churches become toxic when "ungrateful, unholy, unloving, contrary, and critical" comments are allowed to circulate unchecked. When people are "without self-control and brutal, . . . disloyal, reckless, and conceited," leadership becomes dispirited and people walk away (2 Tim 3:2-5). And who can blame them? It is completely contrary to the command of Christ. I'll never forget my first call to ministry: Three months after I arrived as associate pastor, my senior pastor was fired. People were so brutal to him—and to one another—that I dreaded coming to church. I called it "verbal sniper fire in the narthex." I almost left ministry then and there. And I have never forgotten the lesson I learned.

Second, call each other to account, but recognize your own faults first. When people are behaving badly, the church needs to intervene. We are mutually accountable in the household of God. "If a person is caught doing something wrong"—and, since sin lurks and no one is fully sanctified yet, we all will!—"you who are spiritual should restore someone like this" (Gal 6:1). Not every behavior is acceptable. With care for the poor as a central teaching of Jesus, Pope Francis wasn't afraid to call out a bishop dubbed the "Bishop of Bling" for a reported $42 million renovation to his residence, including a $20,000 bathtub, $34,000 conference table, and $4 million chapel.[12] Forbearance with one another does not imply that anything goes.

But when we correct another, it is crucial that we relinquish any spirit of pride or self-righteousness and instead seek an attitude of gentleness and humility. As tempting as it is to tear another down in anger, retaliation, or resentment, when we speak the truth, we speak "the truth with love" (Eph 4:15) and correct "with a spirit of gentleness" (Gal 6:1). Otherwise we succumb to the very sin we abhor. We must watch out for ourselves lest we're tempted too and test our own work (Gal 6:2-4). Though I hate to admit it, when I was caught gossiping about a predecessor, a member of my church quietly called me out on it. He was right, and I'm a better Christian for it.

Third, continually strive for spiritual maturity. Sanctification doesn't happen with the snap of a finger, which is the instant-gratification timetable our culture runs on today. But that doesn't mean it doesn't happen. It is a lifelong process of being loved into our best selves: loved by Christ and loved by his community. I think of being sanctified as something like the image of becoming real in the children's classic *The Velveteen Rabbit*:

"What is REAL?" asked the Rabbit one day, when they were lying side by side near the nursery fender. . . . "Does it mean having things that buzz inside you and a stick-out handle?" "Real isn't how you are made," said the Skin Horse. "It's a thing that happens to you. When a child loves you for a long, long time, not just to play with, but REALLY loves you, then you become Real."

"Does it hurt?" asked the Rabbit. "Sometimes," said the Skin Horse, for he was always truthful. "When you are Real you don't mind being hurt." "Does it happen all at once, like being wound up," he asked, "or bit by bit?"

"It doesn't happen all at once," said the Skin Horse. "You become. It takes a long time. That's why it doesn't happen often to people who break easily, or have sharp edges, or who have to be carefully kept. Generally, by the time you are Real, most of your hair has been loved off, and your eyes drop out and you get loose in the joints and very shabby. But these things don't matter at all, because once you are Real you can't be ugly, except to people who don't understand."[13]

Sanctification, or becoming real, is a lifelong process of being lovingly humbled and corrected and used by God in ways that we may not even understand. Yet we trust that our gifts—even in our shabbiness!—do matter to God. And, bit by bit, we discover what a privilege it is to see our gifts build up others in faith: "The body makes itself grow in that it builds itself up with love as each one does its part" (Eph 4:12-16).

Fourth, when (not if!) there's conflict, start by working it out privately. Gossip and slander are toxic. For generations, parking lot sidebars have escalated private resentments between Christians into factions. These days, it is especially easy to share our grievances through e-mails, Facebook, and Twitter, and their damage goes viral. And it is a dreadful witness to the world to air our dirty laundry.

There is no question that there are times when issues need to go public for the sake of transparency. Too often, church authorities bury financial misdeeds or sexual misconduct without acknowledgment—even sending perpetrators on to another church without comment. But the solution isn't to make *everything* public. Instead, building trustworthy places of truth telling is critical.

In my congregation we try to practice Jesus's instructions: "If your brother or sister sins against you, go and correct them when you are alone together. . . . But if they won't listen, take with you one or two others so that every word may be established by the mouth of two or three witnesses" (Matt 18:15-16). When someone has a grievance, the first step is to go directly to the individual involved. If they don't listen, or if for any reason it doesn't feel safe, then we encourage a third party to help the dialogue. When people feel heard and understood, they are far likelier to stay in community, contributing their gifts and growing in Christ.

The church today faces many difficult conflicts. Just like the early church, we will experience arguments both within congregations and also across ideological, geographic, ethnic, and political divides. The question is not whether they will happen but how we will handle them when they arise. But even in conflict, our approach can confirm the gospel of Jesus Christ. Recently I've witnessed the power of such a witness at work.

In the wake of the 2012 General Assembly (G.A.) of the Presbyterian Church (USA), when commissioners voted to allow non-celibate gays and lesbians to be ordained, over three hundred congregations chose to leave the denomination. At the next G.A. in 2014, delegates voted to permit pastors to conduct same-sex weddings. Those in favor of same-sex unions braced themselves for a backlash. Some conservative groups reacted with an understandable outcry.

But another conservative voice in the church, the Fellowship of Presbyterians and Presbyterians for Renewal, chose a different path. Immediately they sent a public letter. They were honest about their disappointment: "We grieve these actions by the General Assembly. We believe we will look back on this day and see the error." Yet instead of urging revenge or withdrawal from the denomination, they embodied the gospel of reconciliation. They spoke appreciatively of their opponents' work behind the scenes to mediate the conflict: "Proponents [of same-sex marriage] have made great effort to invite and welcome those who hold unwaveringly to a traditional interpretation of marriage to remain engaged in the mission and ministry of the PC(USA) with full integrity." They acknowledged challenges that may still lie ahead: "Some will resolve to do this—others may not. Those of us who do remain in the PC(USA) will, no doubt, encounter other decisions and actions with which we will disagree."

Then they proclaimed the primacy of the gospel over the differences we bear:

> We are not here to fight and divide, but to continue to proclaim the good news of Jesus Christ and to testify to the transforming power of his love that is available to everyone. We urge you in the strongest possible way to refrain from actions, attitudes, and language that would mar the image of Christ in your response to the Assembly's actions.
>
> Let us commit to one another, and to Almighty God, that we will seek to embody the grace and love of our Savior across our theological differences, and in personal and congregational deliberations about our future in the PC(USA).

Truly they are living out the command of Jesus Christ: "Love each other. Just as I have loved you, so you also must love each other. This is how everyone will know that you are my disciples, when you love each other" (John 13:34-35).

Chapter 7

The Path Ahead

Is the church obsolete? Perhaps so, if the church to which we are referring means the church in the form we inherited. The church as we know it was constructed in and for a very different age. For centuries in the West, Christianity was the dominant religion. Everyone was expected to go to church, and the language, values, and habits of Christendom prevailed.

But now we find ourselves in a new age. The global village has arrived.

One of my dearest friends, Denise Schlatter, was a native of Switzerland. A pastor in the Evangelical Reformed Church, she came from a long line of church leaders. Denise's family is well established in Switzerland: for over five hundred years, her family has had a home in their ancestral village in the Swiss Alps.

But Denise's daughter Nora is a citizen of the world. As a teenager, she lived with my family as an exchange student in high school. Later she earned her undergraduate degree at Wellesley College; now she is pursuing her PhD in political science from Columbia University in New York City. Having completed her coursework, she is living back in Zurich now. But this year, Nora will do on-site research in East Timor.

Nora is perfectly at home in her ancestral village. But she feels equally at home anywhere in the world. How will the church reach her generation? Just as the earliest Christians were called to reach the global village of their time, so now are we.

The work that church leaders spend so much time on—preserving church buildings and pipe organs, meeting about curriculum and what to serve at fellowship, arguing about staff vacation policies or the color of the carpet in the sanctuary—will not prove to be important in the long run. The only measure of the ultimate value of the energy we spend is whether it supports our primary calling to be faithful to the gospel of Jesus Christ in this rapidly changing world.

It may feel like a fool's errand to try to reach out to citizens of the global village. It may feel like an overwhelming effort. It is no wonder that we retreat to the tasks with which we are most familiar, supported by the structures and priorities embedded in an earlier age. But there is far more crucial work to be done. I pray we awaken in time to do it.

What is our work at hand? The same tasks that faced our earliest brothers and sisters in faith two thousand years ago. It gives me immense comfort to know that the saints have already laid the path for us. As the fog of cryptomnesia lifts, we begin to remember how that path goes.

Sorting and Sifting

Just like the early Christians, we need to do the work of careful theological sifting within our community: discerning what is central—and what is not—to our inherited faith. Consider what was at stake for the first believers: if they had kept everything they inherited, including circumcision as entry into the covenant, food prohibitions, and the myriad laws related to scripture, custom, and culture, then the gospel would never have taken hold in the Greco-Roman world. It would have been understandable for them to have chosen that route. In a rapidly changing world, their identity was under attack, and they were vulnerable. But to forge ahead, and to stay faithful, they chose to focus whole-heartedly on very few select "essentials":

- loving and worshiping the Lord God alone

- trusting the enduring word of God in scripture

- learning and following the path of Jesus

- committing to shared discernment in the community, led by the Spirit

The rest—including the ages-old covenant practice of circumcision—was considered optional. The clarity over *what* they decided was possible only because of *how* they discerned. They courageously witnessed to the presence of the Spirit in their midst. They listened to one another with mutual forbearance and empathy. They discerned conclusions together, at times painstakingly revisiting the same issues again and again until they were resolved. The process was not easy for them, and the same will be true for us. But it is worth it. For *how* we discern will be crucial in assuring that *what* we discern will fulfill God's will.

Authority within Community

Discernment is no small task in any age, but it is especially complex in times of rapid change. In such a time people question authority and rules that were once presumed, creating discord and uncertainty. Just think of the upheaval created by movable type, which unleashed the modern era and the Reformation. The early church experienced this also, as Roman roads connected people and ideas with unprecedented speed.

The first followers of Jesus were in the midst of a revolution of thought within Judaism. Whether in the halls of power in Jerusalem, the schools of Alexandria, or the urban landscape of Rome, Jewish leaders debated the best way to practice the faith in their changing world. Pharisees, Sadducees, Essenes, Zealots, and others all sought to discern what it means to be faithful—

whether interacting with political powers or practicing the Sabbath, interpreting scripture or worshiping God.

The church today is facing a similar cacophony of competing voices that are offering advice about what Christians should believe and how they should behave. This multiplicity of opinions is to be expected in times of such rapid change. The question, then, is not whether there is disagreement over whose voice has authority, but how to discern faithfully. Today the challenge is two-fold.

First, the pattern of authority in many churches is based on the twentieth-century model of the corporation. Structures are bureaucratic, polity is cumbersome, decision making is slow, and relational trust is low. To move forward, churches can no longer rely on endless committee meetings, votes, and papers. Especially when issues are sensitive, the up/down, win/lose nature of votes can inadvertently interfere with the upbuilding of the church and the unity of faith (Eph 4:12-13).

Second, the institutional church assumption of brand loyalty is long gone. The consumer of religion is more individualistic than ever. "Sheila-ism," as sociologist Robert Bellah dubbed it, is the fastest-growing trend in religion, as people pick and choose whatever they want from among a buffet of spiritual options. Churches and denominations can no longer assume that members have an investment in waiting out prolonged battles or agreeing with official rulings on divisive matters.

What is the church to do? Reclaim the earliest model of authority in our life together: the *ekklesia*, the household of God. However small or large a congregation, the *ekklesia* encourages us to find places where individual gifts are known and shared. Instead of seeking to fulfill committee slots, we seek to fulfill each person's calling within and beyond the church. Instead of measuring the health of the church in numbers—any more than we would measure the health of a family by virtue of its size—we measure our health by the growth in values, maturity, and character of each member. And instead of worrying about preserving the structure of the church the way it was in the "good old days," we focus on the well-being of the family of Christ in our world today.

This does not mean that there is no authority over our actions. We are mutually accountable to one another as "members of one another" (Eph 4:25 NRSV). We are accountable to one another within our community, and we are accountable to the larger church—both within and beyond denominations; both within America and around the world. We measure our maturity against the maturity of Christ as we seek to grow more and more into his likeness. And we strive for our focus to be less about ourselves than about fulfilling Christ's calling: to love the Lord our God with all our hearts and minds and strength and to love our neighbor—and even our enemy—as ourselves.

Cultural Interpreters to the World

Loving our neighbor can take us far beyond our comfort zone. That was certainly Jesus's message to his followers as he told them stories of the good Samaritan (Luke 10:25-37) and prodigal son (Luke 15:11-32), ate with tax collectors (Matt 9:11), and talked with the woman at the well (John 4:6-29). It was also the early church's experience as the Spirit propelled them to partake of unclean foods and baptize Gentiles (Acts 10) and testify to philosophers in Athens (Acts 17:16-33). In retrospect, it is hard for us to imagine the Christian faith unfolding in any other way. But then it was messy and uncomfortable—especially at a time of such unprecedented change, when people longed to find security in the familiar.

Should we be surprised that our calling is messy and uncomfortable too? Yet, if we are to fulfill Christ's call to "go and make disciples of all nations" (Matt 28:19), we must be prepared to do whatever it takes to bring the message to the masses.

We have an advantage the early Christians did not enjoy: we have the retrieved memory that we have done this before. Following the script of the early church, our way is clear.

Our task is not to preserve the institutional church but to go out into the world around us. That mission might take some of us to the ends of the earth. But the vast majority of us have opportunities right outside our doors, at the soccer field or at our desks, on a walk with a friend or in the boardroom.

We may feel ill equipped to do so. Though it is important for us to be as clear about our faith as we can, we do not need to worry about fluency in "church-ese"—the language of theology, erudite philosophy, or expertise in biblical studies. As the early Christians modeled for us, it is far more important that we are fluent in the language of the culture around us and able to articulate our faith in the vernacular of our surroundings.

At times we will interact with people of very different beliefs, values, and traditions. As we do, our job is not to reject or judge them but instead to approach them with respect—even looking for places of mutual agreement.

This does not mean that "all roads lead up the same mountain," as some are inclined to pronounce. As we discern places of agreement, we also come to see places of difference. One of the fruits of the Spirit, for example, is self-control (Gal 5:23)—a very different aspiration than the sensual pleasure and self-gratification touted by many in our culture. And seeking to be Christ-minded through humility (Phil 2:8) is a very different goal than the prizes of fame, power, or fortune promoted in our society. When carrying the message of the gospel, understanding of and respect for others' points of view does not mean agreeing with everybody on every matter.

The method of sharing the gospel matters too. As the earliest Christians learned, it does not hurt to be media savvy. In their time this meant carrying letters on papyrus and holding discussions in the civic arena. Now, it may mean making points on Facebook posts and Pinterest and holding discussions in town halls, at tailgates, or even in taverns.

How we take the message of the gospel out reflects as much on Christ as what we say. If we believe Christlikeness means humility, then we must enact our faith with that spirit. If we believe Christlikeness is manifest in service, then we tell the good news with our generosity to the poor and welcome to the stranger. If we believe that Christlikeness draws us to be stewards of the world God made and "so loves" (John 3:16), then we place a priority on care for the climate and its impact. And if we believe Christlikeness values loving the Lord our God with all our hearts and minds and strength, then we walk the talk by placing worship ahead of youth sports or work demands.

If there is any good news for the future of the church, it is that the millennial generation values integrity and service ahead of individualism. In this season of the church's life, words are not enough to convince the culture. What is required to show *and* tell.

Honoring One Another's Ministries in the Midst of Differences

It is central to our faith to demonstrate love for our neighbors in how we treat the stranger, the poor, the hungry, and the sick. Yet it is no less important to demonstrate love for our neighbors in how we treat each other in the church. This is perhaps the most underrated way that we evidence our faith to the world. Especially at a time when the media focus on conflicts, crises, and ethical lapses in every sphere from the corporate office to the White House, we can predict that the church's dissension and failure will get far more public attention than our success stories. Whether or not that is fair is pointless; it is an aspect of being media savvy. What matters most is to realize that our internecine wars are poisoning the very message of the gospel we hope to convey.

How, then, do we practice what we preach? We begin by sharing clearly and frequently that all of us who call ourselves Christian—liberal and conservative, evangelical and progressive, mainline and emerging, Orthodox, Protestant, and Catholic—share our central faith in Jesus Christ. This is far more than a matter of official pronouncements from church headquarters. It is demonstrated in the day-to-day conversations of ordinary believers.

A corollary is acknowledging that the vast majority of our differences are, in the end, *adiaphora*, "indifferent." This is not to say that they do not matter. Instead, it is to acknowledge that as in the time of the earliest Christians, we will inevitably entertain heartfelt disagreements about numerous matters. Their disagreements included circumcision and eating unclean foods. In later generations disagreements have involved matters as diverse as the authority of the pope, the centrality of scripture, the immorality of slavery, women's ordination, and the place in the church for people who are gay and lesbian. In future generations, there will be other issues that divide us. This will always be the case. But *how* we deal with these differences is crucial.

Like the early Christians, we will do our best when we honor our different expressions while at the same time staying connected. It may seem rote or meaningless to meet with Christians of other stripes. But it is crucial if we are to remain one family in Jesus Christ. We come together to celebrate our deeply rooted connection in Christ and to celebrate what the Spirit is doing in each other's communions. By testifying and listening, we learn from each other and grow in our own faith. And we discover what God is up to far beyond the walls of our own fellowship. It is inspiring.

That does not mean that any behavior in every circumstance is fine. We also come together to discern where boundaries have been crossed. If we are all striving to grow in maturity in Jesus Christ, we need to acknowledge those places where immaturity is winning the day—not just in matters of licentiousness, but also in pride, greed, and not caring about the poor. Sin manifests itself in countless ways; to focus on only one is foolish. Yet, even as we call each other to account, we do well to name our own faults first. Sin is endemic to the human condition, and humility is the first of the fruits of Christ's Spirit.

Looking Backward, Moving Forward

It is amazing how much we have in common with the first Christians. As we reclaim their well-honed tools, we remember how useful they are for our changing world today. And, just as crucially, let us take heart in knowing that we are not the first to have trod this ground.

How easy it is to forget how discouraged the earliest Christians were. Plagued by doubts, troubled by dissension, weary of rejection by the culture, they wondered whether they had mistaken the promise of Jesus Christ. How did they find their way forward? In part, they found their way forward by looking back, recalling the faithfulness of the pioneers in faith who went before them, and remembering the faithfulness of God in every age.

One of my favorite passages in scripture, which we read every All Saints' Day, is this passage from Hebrews 11–12:

> Faith is the reality of what we hope for, the proof of what we don't see. The elders in the past were approved because they showed faith. . . .
>
> By faith Abraham obeyed when he was called to go out to a place that he was going to receive as an inheritance. He went out without knowing where he was going. . . .
>
> By faith Moses refused to be called the son of Pharaoh's daughter when he was grown up. He chose to be mistreated with God's people instead of having the temporary pleasures of sin. . . .
>
> What more can I say? I would run out of time if I told you about Gideon, Barak, Samson, Jephthah, David, Samuel, and the prophets. Through faith they conquered kingdoms, brought about justice, realized promises, shut the mouths of lions, put out raging fires, escaped from the edge of the sword, found strength in weakness, were mighty in war, and routed foreign armies. . . .
>
> But others experienced public shame by being taunted and whipped; they were even put in chains and in prison. They were stoned to death, they were cut in two, and they died by being murdered with swords. They went about wearing the skins of sheep and goats, needy, oppressed, and mistreated.

The world didn't deserve them. They wandered around in deserts, mountains, caves, and holes in the ground. . . .

So then let's also run the race that is laid out in front of us, since we have such a great cloud of witnesses surrounding us. Let's throw off any extra baggage, get rid of the sin that trips us up, and fix our eyes on Jesus, faith's pioneer and perfecter. He endured the cross, ignoring the shame, for the sake of the joy that was laid out in front of him, and sat down at the right side of God's throne. (11:1-2, 8, 24-25, 32-34, 36-38; 12:1-2)

The world is changing fast, and we may not think we know the way. But Jesus, who has led us in the past, will restore our memories to us once more. And he will lead us forward along a faithful path, into the future God has in store.

Notes

Introduction: Cryptomnesia

1. Pew Research Center, "'Nones' on the Rise: One-in-five Adults Have No Religious Affiliation," October 9, 2012, http://www.pewforum.org/files/2012/10/NonesOnTheRise-full.pdf.

1. When Everything Changes

1. Rudyard Kipling, "Sussex," in *Kipling: Poems*, ed. Peter Washington (New York: Everyman's Library, 2007), 116.

2. Gail Anderson Ricciuti (unpublished paper presented to the Moveable Feast Study Group, Colgate Rochester Crozer Divinity School, Rochester, NY, January 2005); portions shortened for oral presentation purposes.

3. Ibid.

4. Alan Millar, "Marshall McLuhan: The Global Village" (interview with Marshall McLuhan), *Explorations*, CBS, May 18, 1960, http://www.cbc.ca/archives/categories/arts-entertainment/media/marshall-mcluhan-the-man-and-his-message/world-is-a-global-village.html, Medium: Television; Program: Explorations; Broadcast.

5. Marshall McLuhan, "Electronic Revolution: Revolutionary Effects of New Media (1959)," in *Understanding Me: Lectures and Interviews* (Cambridge, MA: MIT Press, 2004), 2.

6. Marshall McLuhan, *Understanding Media: The Extensions of Man* (Cambridge, MA: MIT Press, 1994), 5.

7. Eric Schmidt and Jared Cohen, *The New Digital Age: Reshaping the Future of People, Nations and Business* (New York: Knopf, 2013), 3–4.

8. Ibid.

9. Victor Luckerson, "Samsung Just Launched Its Own Music Streaming Service," *Time*, March 7, 2014, http://time.com/16305/samsung-milk-music-streaming-service-launches/.

10. Alan May, in e-mail to author, March 17, 2014.

11. "Best Online Bachelor's Programs," *U.S. News & World Report*, last modified January 24, 2014, http://www.usnews.com/education/online-education/bachelors/rankings?int=a39209.

12. Jane Nelson, "The Operation of Non-Governmental Organisations (NGOs) in a World of Corporate and Other Codes of Conduct," March 2007, Corporate Social Responsibility Initiative, Working Paper No. 34 (Cambridge, MA: John F. Kennedy School of Government, Harvard University), 2.

13. Schmidt and Cohen, *New Digital Age*, 6.

14. Robert N. Bellah, *Habits of the Heart: Individualism and Commitment in American Life* (Berkeley: University of California Press, 2008), 221.

15. Pew Research Center, "'Nones' on the Rise."

16. John Vest, "What Is Post-Christendom?," *Adventures in Post-Christendom* (blog), January 13, 2014, http://johnvest.com/2014/01/13/what-is-post-christendom/.

17. Statistics for 1960 from "Christian Church Membership in the United States: 1960–2002," Demographia.com, http://www.demographia.com/db-religusa2002.htm; 2010 statistics from "Church Giving Drops $1.2 billion Reports 2012 Yearbook of Churches," National Council of Churches News, March 20, 2012, http://ncccusa.org/news/120209yearbook2012.html.

18. Marsha K. Hoover, "On Christmas Eve 1999."

19. Pew Research Center, "'Nones' on the Rise."

20. Diana Butler Bass, *Christianity after Religion: The End of Church and the Birth of a New Spiritual Awakening* (New York: HarperOne, 2013), 5–6.

21. Ricciuti.

2. Religious Life in the Shrinking World

1. "Find Churches in Chicago, IL," WhitePages, accessed June, 3, 2014, http://www.whitepages.com/business?utf8=√&key=church&where=chicago%2C+IL.

2. Nico Hines, "Sunday Assembly Is the Hot New Atheist Church," *Daily Beast*, September 21, 2013, http://www.thedailybeast.com/articles/2013/09/21/sunday -assembly-is-the-hot-new-atheist-church.html.

3. Lincoln Paine, *The Sea and Civilization: A Maritime History of the World* (New York: Knopf, 2013), 56, 79.

4. Wayne Meeks, *The First Urban Christians: The Social World of the Apostle Paul* (New Haven, CT: Yale University Press, 2003), 17.

5. Ibid., 18.

6. Ibid.

7. Paine, *Sea and Civilization*, 132.

8. Diogenes Laertius, *Lives of Eminent Philosophers*, ed. R. D. Hicks (Cambridge, MA: Harvard University Press, 1972), http://www.perseus.tufts.edu/hopper/text?doc =Perseus:text:1999.01.0258.

9. Richard Kraut, "Plato," in *The Stanford Encyclopedia of Philosophy* (Fall 2013 edition), ed. Edward N. Zalta, accessed February 9, 2014, http://plato.stanford.edu /archives/fall2013/entries/plato/.

10. George Karamanolis, "Plutarch," in *The Stanford Encyclopedia of Philosophy* (Fall 2010 ed.), ed. Edward N. Zalta, accessed February 10, 2014, http://plato .stanford.edu/archives/fall2010/entries/plutarch/.

11. Edward Moore, "Gnosticism," in *Internet Encyclopedia of Philosophy*, accessed February 10, 2014, http://www.iep.utm.edu/gnostic/.

12. Dirk Baltzly, "Stoicism," in *The Stanford Encyclopedia of Philosophy* (Spring 2014 ed.), ed. Edward N. Zalta, accessed February 10, 2014, http://plato.stanford .edu/archives/spr2014/entries/stoicism/.

13. Katja Vogt, "Seneca," in *The Stanford Encyclopedia of Philosophy* (Summer 2013 ed.), ed. Edward N. Zalta, accessed February 10, 2014, http://plato.stanford .edu/archives/sum2013/entries/seneca/.

14. Margaret Graver, "Epictetus," in *The Stanford Encyclopedia of Philosophy* (Spring 2013 ed.), ed. Edward N. Zalta, accessed February 10, 2014, http://plato .stanford.edu/archives/spr2013/entries/epictetus/.

15. Richard Parry, "Ancient Ethical Theory," in *The Stanford Encyclopedia of Philosophy* (Fall 2009 ed.), ed. Edward N. Zalta, accessed February 10, 2014, http:// plato.stanford.edu/archives/fall2009/entries/ethics-ancient/.

16. L. Michael White, *From Jesus to Christianity* (San Francisco: HarperCollins, 2004), 49–50.

17. R. E. Witt, *Isis in the Ancient World* (Baltimore: Johns Hopkins University Press, 1997).

18. *Encyclopaedia Britannica Online*, s.v. "Mithra," accessed February 10, 2014, http://www.britannica.com/EBchecked/topic/386025/Mithra.

19. White, *From Jesus to Christianity*, 53–55.

20. Philo, *De Specialibus Legibus* i.319f, in *The New Testament Background*, rev. ed., ed. C. K. Barrett (San Francisco: Harper & Row, 1987), 268.

21. White, *From Jesus to Christianity*, 76.

22. Philo, *De Specialibus*, in Barrett, *New Testament Background*, 204.

23. *Encyclopaedia Britannica Online*, s.v. "sanhedrin," accessed February 10, 2014, http://www.britannica.com/EBchecked/topic/522434/sanhedrin.

24. Julie Galambush, *The Reluctant Parting: How the New Testament's Jewish Writers Created a Christian Book* (San Francisco: HarperCollins, 2005), 9.

25. Ibid.

26. Josephus, *War* ii, in Barrett, *New Testament Background*, 159.

27. Ibid.

28. Galambush, *Reluctant Parting*, 9–10.

29. Josephus, *War* ii, in Barrett, *New Testament Background*, 158.

30. Ibid.

31. Galambush, *Reluctant Parting*, 10.

32. Ibid.

33. Felix Just, "Jewish Groups at the Time of Jesus," Electronic New Testament Educational Resources, last modified October 19, 2001, http://catholic-resources .org/Bible/Jewish_Groups.htm#Scribes.

34. Galambush, *Reluctant Parting*, 10–11.

3. Sifting Our Inheritance

1. Phyllis Tickle, *The Great Emergence: How Christianity Is Changing and Why* (Grand Rapids: Baker, 2012), 16.

2. Barrett, *New Testament Background*, 204, emphasis mine.

3. Meeks, *First Urban Christians*, 80.

4. David E. Garland, "The Dispute Over Food Sacrificed to Idols (1 Cor 8:1-11:1)," accessed February 20, 2014, http://www.vanderbilt.edu/AnS/religious_stud ies/SNTS2002/garland.htm.

5. "Tractate 'Abodah Zarah," in *Babylonian Talmud*, Folio 29a, accessed February 20, 2014, http://www.come-and-hear.com/zarah/zarah_29.html.

6. Summary of B. Yevamot 46a, found in Lawrence H. Schiffman, *Who Was a Jew? Rabbinic and Halakhic Perspectives on the Jewish-Christian Schism* (Brooklyn, NY: KTAV Publishing, 1985), 33.

7. "When Everything Is Important, Nothing Is Important," *Extreme Clutter with Peter Walsh*, accessed May 15, 2014, http://www.oprah.com/own-extreme-clutter-peter-walsh/When-Everything-is-Important-Nothing-is-Important; and "When the Cameras Went Off," *Extreme Clutter with Peter Walsh*, accessed March 25, 2014, http://www.oprah.com/own-extreme-clutter-peter-walsh/When-the-Cameras-Went-Off.

8. Jan Edmiston, "Embracing Spiritual Climate Change" *achurchforstarving artists* (blog), March 26, 2014, http://achurchforstarvingartists.wordpress.com/2014/03/26/embracing-spiritual-climate-change/.

9. See, e.g., Thomas G. Long, *Beyond the Worship Wars* (Washington, DC: Alban Institute, 2001).

10. Stephen Miller, "The Modern Worship Music Wars," *Relevant*, August 29, 2013, http://www.relevantmagazine.com/god/church/modern-worship-music-wars#mdKfhtmojCwDfczr.99.

11. Michael Jinkins, "Intellectual Empathy," *Call & Response Blog* (blog), March 6, 2012, http://www.faithandleadership.com/blog/03-05-2012/michael-jinkins-intellectual-empathy.

12. Ibid.

13. Bill Tammeus, "A Pastor's Epiphany on Gays," *Bill's 'Faith Matters' Blog* (blog), March 13, 2014, http://billtammeus.typepad.com/my_weblog/2014/03/3-13-14.html.

4. Authority and Community in a Flattened Age

1. Lev Grossman, "Iran Protests: Twitter, the Medium of the Movement," *Time*, June 17, 2009, http://content.time.com/time/world/article/0,8599,1905125,00.html.

2. "I Am Malala: The Girl Who Stood Up for Education and Was Shot by the Taliban," Goodreads.com, accessed February 21, 2014, http://www.goodreads.com/book/show/17851885-i-am-malala.

3. Schmidt and Cohen, *New Digital Age*, 4.

4. Ibid., 3.

5. Halimah Abdullah, "Obama Interrupted: Disrespectful or Latest in 'Era of Incivility'?," CNN.com, June 15, 2012, http://www.cnn.com/2012/06/15/politics/obama-interrupted/.

6. Schmidt and Cohen, *New Digital Age*, 3.

7. Thomas L. Friedman, *The World Is Flat* (New York: Picador, 2007), 238.

8. Ibid.

9. Pew Research Center, "'Nones' on the Rise."

10. Butler Bass, *Christianity after Religion*, 66–67.

11. Friedman, *World Is Flat*, 238.

12. Galambush, *Reluctant Parting*, 10–11.

13. A. H. Armstrong, *An Introduction to Ancient Philosophy* (Totowa, NJ: Rowman & Allanheld, 1983), 115.

14. Barrett, *New Testament Background*, 254.

15. Meeks, *First Urban Christians*, 80–81.

16. Ibid., 77.

17. Ibid.

18. Ibid., 78–79.

19. Ibid., 83.

20. Ibid., 86.

21. Bellah, *Habits of the Heart*, 221.

22. Robert N. Bellah, "Habits of the Heart" (lecture, St. Mark's Catholic Church, Isla Vista, CA, February 21, 1986), http://www.robertbellah.com/lectures_5.htm.

23. Schmidt and Cohen, *New Digital Age*, 3–4.

24. Friedman, *World Is Flat*, 238.

25. Butler Bass, *Christianity after Religion*, 72.

26. Ibid.

27. Ibid.

28. John C. Dorhauer, "Church 3.0," *The Blue Yarn* (blog), February 14, 2014, http://theblueyarn.com/2014/02/14/church-3-0/.

29. Frank Yamada, personal correspondence, June 2, 2014.

30. Armstrong, *Introduction to Ancient Philosophy*, 115.

31. "Boost Your Talents with Clifton StrengthsFinder," Gallup Strengths Center, accessed April 7, 2014, https://www.gallupstrengthscenter.com/Purchase/en-US/Index.

32. Theresa Latini, *The Church and the Crisis of Community: A Practical Theology of Small Group Ministry* (Grand Rapids: Eerdmans, 2011), 5.

33. Ibid., 180–81.

34. Shane Stanford, "Why Are Our Churches So Empty?," *Making Life Matter* (blog), February 22, 2014, http://www.shanestanfordmlm.com/1/post/2014/02/why-are-our-churches-so-empty.html.

35. Meeks, *First Urban Christians*, 146.

36. Peter Marty, quoted by Amy Frykholm, "Loose Connections: What's Happening to Church Membership?," *Christian Century*, May 16, 2011, http://www.christiancentury.org/article/2011-05/loose-connections.

37. "St. Teresa of Avila," Archdiocese of Dublin Education Secretariat, accessed June 2, 2014, http://education.dublindiocese.ie/st-teresa-of-avila/.

5. Taking the Message to the Masses

1. James Emery White, "Reaching Out to the Unchurched," *Church and Culture* (blog), August 20, 2012, http://www.churchandculture.org/Blog.asp?ID=3201.

2. Phyllis Tickle, "The Shift into Post-Christendom," *Emergent Village* (blog), October 5, 2012, http://www.patheos.com/blogs/emergentvillage/2012/10/the-shift-into-post-christendom/. She cites Stuart Murray's *Post-Christendom: Church and Missions in a Strange New World* (Carlisle, UK: Paternoster, 2004), 83–84, as reproduced by Lloyd Pietersen in *Reading the Bible after Christendom* (Harrisonburg, VA: Herald Press, 2012).

3. John Vest, "Where Is Your City on the Post-Christendom Continuum?," *Adventures in Post-Christendom* (blog), January 15, 2014, http://johnvest.com/2014/01/15/where-is-your-city-on-the-post-christendom-continuum/.

4. "The Most Post-Christian Cities," Barna Group, accessed June 2, 2014, http://cities.barna.org/the-most-post-christian-cities-in-america/.

5. Paine, *Sea and Civilization*, 132.

6. Tom Standage, "Social Media? It's Not a New Idea. Try Following Cicero and Caesar's Feeds," *Wired*, December 3, 2013, http://www.wired.co.uk/magazine/archive/2013/11/play/youre-so-passe-zuck/viewgallery/329948.

7. Claire Trageser, "Ardent Atheists Spread Their Reverence for Disbelief," NPR, February 26, 2014, http://www.npr.org/2014/02/26/281450206/ardent-atheists-spread-their-reverence-for-disbelief.

8. "A History of the Parliament," Council for a Parliament of the World's Religions, accessed February 28, 2014, https://www.parliamentofreligions.org/.

9. "Program Archives," *30 Good Minutes*, accessed May 16, 2014, http://www.csec.org/index.php/archives. See Sherre Hirsch, "One God—Part 1," Program 5319, first broadcast February 14, 2010, http://www.csec.org/index.php/archives/23-member-archives/103-sherre-hirsch-program-5319; Eboo Patel, "One God—Part 2," Program 5320, first broadcast February 21, 2010, http://www.csec.org/index.php/archives/23-member-archives/104-eboo-patel-program-5320; and Christine Chakoian, "One God—Part 3," Program 5321, first broadcast February 28, 2010, http://www.csec.org/index.php/archives/23-member-archives/105-christine-chakoian-program-5321.

10. Laurie Goodstein, "An Effort to Foster Tolerance in Religion," *New York Times*, June 13, 2011, http://www.nytimes.com/2011/06/14/us/14patel.html?pagewanted=all. See also "About Eboo," Interfaith Youth Core, accessed May 16, 2014, http://www.ifyc.org/about-us/eboo-patel.

11. Jen Hatmaker, *Seven: An Experimental Mutiny against Excess* (Nashville: B&H Publishing, 2012), 80–82.

12. Jan Edmiston, "What about an Associate Pastor for Neighborhood Ministries?," *achurchforstarvingartists* (blog) April 10, 2014, http://achurchforstarvingartists.wordpress.com/2014/04/10/what-about-an-associate-pastor-for-neighborhood-ministries/.

13. Red Pine, trans., *The Zen Teaching of Bodhidharma* (New York: North Point Press, 1987), 37.

14. *Merriam-Webster OnLine*, s.v. "karma," accessed February 28, 2014, http://www.merriam-webster.com/dictionary/karma.

15. Pope Francis, "Homily of Pope Francis at the Concluding Mass of World Youth Day 2013 on Copacabana Beach" (homily, Rio de Janeiro, July 28, 2013), World Youth Day Central, http://wydcentral.org/final-mass-with-pope-francis-on-copacabana/.

16. Pope Francis, "Evangelii Gaudium (The Joy of the Gospel): Apostolic Exhortation on the Proclamation of the Gospel in Today's World," November 24, 2013, accessed February 28, 2014, http://www.vatican.va/holy_father/francesco/apost_exhortations/documents/papa-francesco_esortazione-ap_20131124_evangelii-gaudium_en.html.

17. Pope Francis, Twitter posts, February 25, 2014, 2:25 a.m.; and February 6, 2014, 3:06 a.m., https://twitter.com/Pontifex.

18. Tracy Connor, "'Who Am I to Judge?' The Pope's Most Powerful Phrase in 2013," NBC News, December 22, 2013, http://www.nbcnews.com/news/world/who-am-i-judge-popes-most-powerful-phrase-2013-v21984495.

19. *Time* magazine, December 23, 2013; *Rolling Stone*, February 12, 2014.

20. Carey Nieuwhof, "7 Ways to Respond as People Attend Church Less Often," *CareyNieuwhof.com* (blog), April 3, 2013, http://careynieuwhof.com/2013/04/7-ways-to-respond-as-people-attend-church-less-often/

21. Ibid.

22. Butler Bass, *Christianity after Religion*, 57–59.

23. Kathleen D. Vohl et al, "Decision Fatigue Exhausts Self-Regulatory Resources—But So Does Accommodating to Unchosen Alternatives," accessed June 26, 2014, http://chicagobooth.edu/research/workshops/marketing/archive/Workshop Papers/vohs.pdf.

6. Can't We All Just Get Along?

1. "Fight Erupts in Jerusalem Church," BBC News, April 20, 2008, http://news.bbc.co.uk/2/hi/middle_east/7357496.stm, published 2008/04/20.

2. Ashley Powers, "An Unforgiving Power Struggle at a Los Feliz Church," *Los Angeles Times*, July 16, 2012, http://articles.latimes.com/2012/jul/16/local/la-me-church-fight-20120716.

3. Morgan Feddes, "TBN Embroiled in 'Sordid' Family Lawsuit," Christianity Today, February 17, 2012, http://www.christianitytoday.com/gleanings/2012/february/tbn-embroiled-in-sordid-family-lawsuit.html.

4. "Two Special Generations: The Millennials and the Boomers," National Conference on Citizenship, accessed March 1, 2014, http://ncoc.net/226.

5. Thom Rainer, "The Millennials Are Rejecting Fighting Churches and Christians," *Thom S. Rainer* (blog), October 21, 2013, http://thomrainer.com/2013/10/21/the-millennials-are-rejecting-fighting-churches-and-christians/.

6. Peter Kirby, "St. Ignatius of Antioch to the Smyrnaeans (Roberts-Donaldson translation)," Early Christian Writings, accessed March 1, 2014, http://www.earlychristianwritings.com/text/ignatius-smyrnaeans-roberts.html.

7. "A Love without Condition," History of the Early Church, accessed March 1, 2014, http://www.earlychurch.com/unconditional-love.php.

8. "The Apostolic Fathers with Justin Martyr and Irenaeus," Christian Classics Ethereal Library, accessed May 19, 2014, http://www.ccel.org/ccel/schaff/anf01.viii.ii.xiv.html.

9. Clement of Alexandria, "Exhortation to the Heathen," in *The Ante-Nicene Fathers*, ed. Philip Schaff, vol. 2, Fathers of the Second Century: Hermas, Tatian,

Athenagoras, Theophilus, and Clement of Alexandria (Grand Rapids: Christian Classics Ethereal Library, 1885), 1159, http://www.ccel.org/ccel/schaff/anf02.pdf.

10. Tertullian, *Apologeticus*, trans. T. R. Glover and Gerald H. Rendall, xxxix, 6–11 (Cambridge, MA: Harvard University Press, 1931), 176–77: *"Vide, inquiunt, ut invicem se diligant; ipsi enim invicem oderunt: et ut pro alterutro mori sint parati; ipsi enim ad occidendum alterutrum paratiores erunt."* "'Look,' they say, 'how they love one another' (for themselves hate one another); 'and how they are ready to die for each other' (for themselves will be readier to kill each other)."

11. N. T. Wright, "What Is the Main Problem in the Western Church?," interview by Jefferson Bethke, "Ask a Leader" series, December 16, 2013, https://www.youtube.com/watch?v=ElLsLBJ_Nvs, transcribed by the author.

12. Charles McPhedran, "Vatican Suspends German 'Bishop of Bling,'" *USA Today*, October 23, 2013, http://www.usatoday.com/story/news/world/2013/10/23/german-bishop-bling-vatican-suspension/3169723/.

13. Margery Williams, *The Velveteen Rabbit: Or How Toys Become Real* (Garden City, NY: Doubleday, 1922), http://digital.library.upenn.edu/women/williams/rabbit/rabbit.html.

CPSIA information can be obtained at www.ICGtesting.com
Printed in the USA
LVOW13s1925310714

396947LV00004B/4/P